JUST MAKE MONEY!

The Entrepreneur's Handbook to:
Building the Life of Your Dreams

ERIC CASABURI

Founder & CEO of
FIERCE BRANDS LLC/RetroFitness, LLC

For more information contact:
FIERCE BRANDS LLC/RetroFitness, LLC
EricCasaburi.com

Hardcover: 978-0-692-41337-1
eBook: 978-0-692-41336-4

Library of Congress Control Number: 2015936876

*I'd like to dedicate this book
to all the self starters who took the risk,
are taking the risk,
and who will continue to take a risk
on a new business in the future.
You make the business world go round.*

CONTENTS

Acknowledgments

I want to thank my wife and kids for their constant and never-ending support of my success...for accepting the additional hours it took away from our family time to make it all happen.

I also want to acknowledge the executive team at Fierce Brands for their tenacity for success as we keep learning and teaching some of the finest business lessons for entrepreneurial success.

CHAPTER ONE

Entrepreneurship— It's Your Driving Force

THE TERM *entrepreneurship* has many definitions and means different things to different individuals, but when you think about the spirit of the entrepreneur, first and foremost, you think about his or her driving passion. Passion is embedded into the entrepreneur's DNA; it defines who they are as a person; they are wired with it.

Job security for most people is provided by their employer (or so they think); entrepreneurs on the other hand, provide job security for *themselves!* This profound way of thinking is innate to the successful entrepreneur.

The passion that fuels every entrepreneur can be acquired with practice. If the thought of being free to call your own shots and amass your own wealth appeals to you, there are skills and values you can learn starting today, with this book. And while hundreds of books on entrepreneurship have been written, none of them tackles the deepest truths about what it takes to successfully run your own show, and to get to that stage as quickly and effectively as possible. In this author's mind, there is no such thing as warming up slowly, and there is no such thing as too big and successful too soon.

That said, being an entrepreneur requires stamina too. If entrepreneurial passion propels you to action, cultivating certain habits will help you over the long run. A fundamental driving force will push you when you don't want to walk anymore, and the same force will push you even harder when you don't want to run. You'll need that inner fuel of enthusiasm. Good things *and* bad things will happen as your business grows, but because you've got that drive and enthusiasm, you'll find the things you need to fix, and you'll fix them.

If you have enough "why," you'll find the "how" to get the solutions you need. I learned this tidbit early on from Anthony Robbins.

The entrepreneur starts out with the simple notion, "I know *I* wish I had this, and I know my customer wishes *he* had this. I want this, and I want to make this happen."

When we think of some of the most successful innovators, past and present—Steve Jobs, Mark Zuckerberg, Ray Kroc, Howard Schultz—what do they have in common? They all saw something consumers needed *before consumers knew they needed it.* They all were extremely resourceful, or became so, because enthusiasm to provide something utterly necessary and unique drove them. Don't think for a moment that these well-known entrepreneurs didn't face obstacles—major obstacles. Indeed they did—we all do. But passion inspires perseverance in business.

As a young entrepreneur myself, I quickly became extremely resourceful, not because I knew everything and had everything; on the contrary, I did not know or have very much. I did not have a college education, nor did I have a ton of money and resources at my fingertips. Fifteen years ago, I didn't have a fraction of the tools I have in my bag today. So what did I do? I did everything short of begging, stealing, or borrowing to acquire them. I also quickly acquired the equivalent of a master's degree by immersing myself in books and periodicals, and by attending as many in-person interviews and seminars as my free time allowed. This meant a ton of late-night reading and writing sessions after my wife and kids were already in bed! Fueled by passion and enthusiasm, I made my way.

Let me give you an example of how your mind needs to operate: If a doctor told you today that you had a serious illness, odds are you would go get a second opinion, and then you'd begin to talk to every single person you know about your condition. You would track down every single resource, study every detail about every possible cure, and take every action you could take that would help you to survive. Right?

In business, as an entrepreneur, you should do the exact same thing, because business is about surviving until you become the predator. Until you are that predator, you are just prey. Business is Darwinian to the core, and sadly, people too often forget that hard fact. Business is survival of the fittest, and the fittest people are the most resourceful, spirited, and adaptable. People who utilize all their resources and possess the passion to thrive and survive will always find and create the ideal environment in which to succeed.

> **...your enthusiasm and experience as an entrepreneur will take you much further than your degree—it will take you as far as you want to go.**

People who observe and learn how other businesses run will have a distinct advantage. My wife laughs at me because when I go to a store or a restaurant, or even when I am watching a commercial on TV, I'm not like most people—I am constantly analyzing what is happening from a business perspective. In my mind, as I watch technology get faster and cheaper, I realize everyone should be figuring out their next career move and planning for their future financial security, and they should be figuring it out now. I worry about those who have nothing set, or who aren't paying close attention to the current state of affairs.

The experience of developing the entrepreneurial spirit is more important now than it ever has been. It is just as important, if not more important, as where you went to school. Sure, if your resume shows that you graduated from West Point or MIT, you've earned some bonus points; but the fact is, your enthusiasm and experience as an entrepreneur will take you much further than your degree—it will take you as far as you want to go.

Our nation is a trillion dollars in debt at the time this book is going to print, so what does that say about what our schools have been teaching about money? It's not the entrepreneurs who have put us in debt; it's the "book-smart" people who have been looking at formulas and spreadsheets and making unwise decisions and predictions. These people couldn't run a lemonade stand and make two nickels in profit on a hot summer's day. Yet we allow them to run the business of our country … and I will say again and again, yes, that too is a business.

A success story begins the day someone decides to take action and get started in business—the kind of business that brings customers something they hadn't yet realized they wanted. Somebody reading this book right now is about to break free and break through toward success—you may still be in school, or you may be stuck in an unpromising job that is just a way to keep from going broke. Or you may already be an entrepreneur, but one who isn't quite making it. Or it could be that you have been a fairly successful entrepreneur, but now you are losing fuel and altitude, and you are sputtering.

Everyone holding this book has probably come to it as a guide for taking a leap of faith—whether it's your first or your fiftieth. And entrepreneurship, to some degree, does require a leap of faith.

Anyone who has started their own business, whether it is a hamburger stand or a landscape company, finds there are many things that can go wrong—or rather, that there are many things they can *do* wrong. The landscape crew that cuts your yard, for example, could just show up in ripped-up t-shirts or soiled clothes—many landscape crews do. But what if a crew showed up in $25 collar-embroidered shirts and khakis? What if the owner of this landscape company made a $25–$50 investment for each of his employees? The attention they would get from people driving by would be positive and substantial. Recognizing "curb appeal" is critical in ALL businesses.

The problem is, too many business owners don't possess that extra special quality of enthusiasm, and this prevents them from selling themselves better. True entrepreneurs, on the other hand, know they are always in sales—they are always promoting their products because they are always on stage. Entrepreneurs are always representing their brand because that's who they are—remember, it is in their DNA, their wiring, and their identity. The entrepreneur is the brand, and the brand is the entrepreneur. A so-so landscaping business owner doesn't realize that if a guy drives by and sees a crew in uniforms instead ripped-up t-shirts, this guy might stop and say, "Wow, this company must be sharp. I would pay them more to do my lawn, because if they care so much about small details, they will treat my property with the same care." Your customer or future customer is always analyzing your product and service at every level, whether consciously or subconsciously. Invest in a company uniform so that when clients drive by, they see a set of unified professionals, not a bunch of laborers. Get the difference in that statement? The successful entrepreneur is on to these types of details. He or she knows that training the landscape crew to politely greet customers goes a long way toward ensuring future success.

> A successful entrepreneur cannot stop doing what he or she loves doing—they can't turn off the meter. Most entrepreneurs learn to manage that meter, but sometimes e-mails get sent in the middle of the night, and sometimes notes are scribbled on napkins—the entrepreneur is never truly "off."

A successful entrepreneur cannot stop doing what he or she loves doing—they can't turn off the meter. Most entrepreneurs learn to manage that meter, but sometimes e-mails

get sent in the middle of the night, and sometimes notes are scribbled on napkins—the entrepreneur is never truly "off." Even a leisurely trip to the bookstore involves research. Maybe you own a hip grilled-cheese food cart in downtown Brooklyn and all is going better than expected, but when you hit the bookstore you can't help but pick up a few books about other businesses. You are on the alert for examples of people who have excelled in their industries—you are always interested and always learning, always hungry and tireless.

As a thoughtful entrepreneur, you are always asking, "How can I transfer that great idea to my business?" or "How can I ensure that my business never turns a blind eye to this need or to that one?" In your downtime, you never stop. Even if you are out to dinner, you are observing the hostess—is she smiling and engaging? Was she properly trained or not trained at all? Was the wait staff hired simply because they are young and attractive, or are they good communicators?

There are substantial differences in the little details that render a business successful or doomed, and as an entrepreneur, your enthusiasm for your product, your brand, and your way of life means you cannot stop observing.

> **Obstacles and challenges anger the entrepreneur, and if you aren't angry enough, perhaps you are not enthusiastic or passionate enough about your business.**

On this same train of thought, when you see other business owners encountering obstacles, and particularly when you encounter your own trials and tribulations, your heart pounds, you start to sweat, and you can't clear it from your mind. Any entrepreneur worth his or her salt becomes enraged when they hear "No," or "That's impossible," or "Maybe later." Rage is a much-criticized word, but this entrepreneur is here to tell you that it is very much part of the necessary fuel. When times get tough, rage can motivate you.

Obstacles and challenges anger the entrepreneur, and if you aren't angry enough, perhaps you are not enthusiastic or passionate enough about your business. Aggression helps you to keep pushing. Powerful emotions drive you to find every resource available, so that you can overcome problems. One

of my mentors has said many times that the drive to avoid pain is much greater than the drive to obtain pleasure. Pain and challenge are good!

There is no easy path to owning a successful business, and when you are on the path, you will face pitfalls—everybody does. Challenges will find you, and they will keep your juices flowing. In fact, often these challenges will serve to widen your perspective, because when you are trying to figure out how to overcome a particular challenge, you may find yourself and your team exploring unchartered territory, and the solutions you find may lead to new products and service possibilities. A challenge may be the remedy that saves your business and propels it forward—if handled correctly.

I am not a fan of the notion that it's dangerous for a business to grow too quickly. If you are an intelligent, due-diligence invested entrepreneur or business owner, understand that you CAN grow quickly—if you use the resources that allow for quick growth. In my opinion, growing too slowly is more dangerous, because the more time you allow your competitors to get into the market before you, the more of your market share they'll acquire.

When going to market, you must enter with full gusto, and shut the gates behind you. An entrepreneur should always watch out for competitors trying to slip in under the gate, and should always hear that clock ticking. Even with my successes, sweat appears on my brow when I think about breaking into new markets. Some might call me insane; I call myself enthusiastic.

Sure, as an entrepreneur, you may sometimes need to assess your enthusiasm. You need to recognize what you do well and what you don't do well, and delegate. Not that there is anything wrong with control—like enthusiasm and speed, control is an essential element of entrepreneurship. But once you realize that you've got an employee who is as good as you at managing the cash register, you should free yourself to go out into the world to spend more time researching, meeting with potential customers, or marketing and visiting possible new locations—whatever it is you need to expand upon.

> **"You can't be working on your business if you are working *in* your business every day."**

We tell all our franchisees, "You can't be working *on* your business if you are working *in* your business every day." This approach puts things into perspective.

Being an entrepreneur begins with acceptance of the fact you can never turn that aspect of yourself off—you are forthright, and your enthusiasm is unstoppable. A doctor at a cocktail party has to assume he will be asked to give medical advice to at least a handful of guests during the course of the night if his profession is made known. You, as a business owner, will never stop talking about your work, because it is not just "work," or a "job"; it is your passion, it is who you are, and it is 24/7. This means that you need to surround yourself with people who understand and support your enthusiasm.

At most social functions and family gatherings, talk eventually will turn to business. This doesn't mean you won't talk about sports or politics or entertainment—of course you will—but because you can't help loving what you do, it will eventually bleed through into conversation: "How'd you do this month?" "How many members did you sign up?" "Hey, how is your juice bar doing? How many smoothies did you sell?" These are just some of the things you will overhear at our house during Thanksgiving dinner.

This is the real deal. This is how it is. You want to own a business and you want to make money owning a business. You are not investing your hard-earned money just to hang

your name on a door. You are taking this gigantic leap of faith because you want to be successful. You want some financial and professional freedom. To achieve all of this requires personality, drive, passion,

If you want to run the race, get your best sneakers on.

and enthusiasm. You have to want to win. If you want to run the race, get your best sneakers on.

My closing statement every time I finish speaking with new potential candidates at an open house for my franchise,

Retro Fitness, is this: "Every morning when you wake up, if you don't feel like you can't wait for your feet to hit the ground because want to sprint to where you are going today, you are in the wrong business, job, or place. Every day, you should be excited to wake up and get to what you're doing. Even if there's a problem, you have got to want to race to get there and fix it, because you want your business to be the best in the world."

TAKEAWAY

- If you dream of a better life that offers you more freedom and more control over your own destiny, then you need to follow your passion into the world of entrepreneurship.

  What are you passionate about? What do you think about constantly, no matter what else you may be doing?

CHAPTER TWO

We Get People What They Didn't Even Know They Could Have

PEOPLE WALK through the front doors of Retro Fitness and they think, *OK, I've gotta work out. I've gotta sweat. I've gotta lose some weight, put on some muscle, run this treadmill, do some circuit training.* A lot of people will come in and plug in their headphones and get moving to the music they carry with them everywhere on their phone. Others come in and turn on their favorite TV show, or catch up on the day's news. Watching everyone do their own thing, whether it is a quick solo workout on a lunch break or a group-fitness workout, you realize that just ten years ago, the gym scene looked totally different. Most people back then took their gym experience for granted and had no idea what lay in store.

Ten years ago, one or two tube TVs (you guys remember those, right?) might have been hooked up on a shelf high on a wall, or a couple of lousy speakers might be playing mono radio—with commercials. Sure, you might have been a little ahead of the curve and gone to the gym carrying your Walkman with your workout mix tape that took you hours to make; but back then, you had no idea how quickly technology would improve your gym experience—and save hours of your life!

These days, as is the case with so many other aspects of our lives, Retro Fitness provides a much more personalized

experience. That nine-hundred-pound tube TV on the wall shelf has become a totally different beast. When it came down off the wall, it was attached to the rack above your treadmill, then it was attached to the treadmill itself, and now—at Retro Fitness—TVs are integrated into the dashboard of the equipment itself. What more could you want? We'll tell you: in the near future, you'll have On Demand entertainment that will link up via the Cloud with whatever you've got lined up in your home system queue. This means no more preset menu for you; no more tiring of your own song lists—you can try something new! Yes, we are bringing you the best of your own world On Demand. You didn't think I'd sit still when it came to revolutionizing the workout, did you?

It's insane how much technology is improving our life experiences—whether we are buying a new Tesla electric car from our iPad (which I did!), or enrolling in a Retro Fitness summer boot camp class from the same device. Our customers are saying, "Wow, this is awesome!" and we feel the same way.

We are proud to offer the best of the best—the latest of the latest. We are proud to teach our clients not just how to use our gym equipment, but also how to utilize our technology, which will help them achieve their fitness goals. For example, we have an app that clients use to find the Retro Fitness location and Retro Fitness class schedule that is most convenient to them. Our clients can track their workouts with their own wearable devices, and the data can sync to our Cloud-based personal fitness dashboard as well, so no mile or step or calorie is ever lost.

There are goals, rewards, and social engagement options as well. Within the dashboard you can choose a goal "Challenge," such as, "I want to run ten miles this week or burn five hundred calories each workout session," and the workout data is then tracked. When you reach your goals, Retro Fitness gives you "Reward Points" that can be redeemed for merchandise. These "Challenges" can be shared via social media too, so your friends can cheer you on or even compete with you!

Today's customers have the option to integrate some serious technology into their routines. Walt Disney always said you don't build it for yourself; you find out what people want and you build it for them. At my company, we constantly stay one step ahead of what our customers might want next—and we are doing this brainstorming while they are crosstraining away their stress in one of our group classes or pumping up their biceps during the FOX Business News brief.

So what's the flip side? Sometimes, as every entrepreneur knows, you get it wrong—maybe you offer a product or a service that, for whatever reason, customers never latch on to. This is bound to happen when you live by what I call "the law of business anticipation." Let me digress a bit here.

Here is a very well kept business secret of some of the best companies and smartest people in the world: They understand the risk involved in taking an entrepreneurial leap of faith, and they love the reward. Nobody talks about the products Steve Jobs and Apple created that weren't as life-altering as the first iPod. Most people have never even heard of the Apple Lisa (yes, that was the name of one of the early Apple computers). In addition to its unfortunate name, the Lisa also had a hefty price tag—in 1983 it sold for $10,000 per unit. Jobs, as most of us know, was asked to leave Apple, which he did. Of course, he eventually returned, and the rest is history. Pretty much every thing Jobs touched after that turned to gold.

Anticipating what the market, customer, and world may need gives you the opportunity to create the next iPhone, PayPal, or Uber. When you get it right, when you manage to anticipate and provide what customers want before they know they want it, you hit a home run. Innovative companies never stop anticipating what their customers will want tomorrow.

When you sell one of the most difficult products in the world, like I do—I sell sweat and pain (let that sink in for a moment!)—you really are working against a deep-set ideology. People want to look good and they want to feel good—but as many of us know, reaching these goals can be challenging physically, emotionally, and mentally. People want to look better in a bathing suit, or they want a healthier heart, and they know they'll have to endure some pain in order to

> **Help your customers stay their course. They have their goals; you have yours—make sure those goals are aligned and merge at the intersection of your product and business.**

succeed and achieve their goals. So in a way, if I truly want my customers to succeed in achieving their personal goals, I have to make part of my business *the business of distraction.*

Entertaining yourself through the pain certainly helps—keep your customers busy and maybe they won't feel the short-term pain as much, or at least it won't consume their focus and discourage them from coming back tomorrow. Keeping customers stimulated, giving them options, and engaging them in the environment that is your gym—or your business space—is crucial. When the product you are selling involves sweat and muscle aches, you need to make sure your customers feel welcome. They should experience a pleasurable environment where they can approach any employee with questions, and where they can order something nutritious and rewarding on their way out the door.

Help your customers stay their course. They have their goals; you have yours—make sure those goals are aligned and merge at the intersection of your product and business.

Commitment and consistency count for the people who come into our fitness centers. We greet our members when they enter, and we say goodbye to them when they leave. This gesture may seem simple, but it makes our customers feel acknowledged, and that makes them happy.

In the fitness industry—and in other service industries as well—we have to stay current for our customers. We have to make sure they have a great experience the whole time they are inside our place of business—every single time. We have to provide them with a consistently great experience that keeps them as committed to us as we are to them. We have to do whatever it takes to ensure that when they walk out our front doors, they are going to tell someone how nice the experience was at Retro Fitness that day.

It's the "Raving Fans" theory. Raving Fans are the customers who absolutely adore your product or services. They are evangelists for your company who tell all their friends and family how wonderful their experience with your company is. They will never leave you, provided you maintain the level of product service that got you into their hearts.

One of our main aims in being committed and consistent is to help customers stay committed and consistent in their workout goals. When our members feel and see the results they have been working so hard for—sweating and burning and aching for weeks and months, especially in the beginning—that's a great source of pride for our team. Our business works well when people succeed with their workout goals. But of course, it doesn't end with the perfect six-pack or an achieved number of miles on a treadmill. Fitness is an ongoing process. So, unlike many industries, we have to sell our customers that pain over and over and over again. Smile if you don't have to do this!

You have to follow up with your customers and clients. It's easy for people to change their opinion about your product, especially in a heavily competitive environment. In our business, even the heartiest New Year's Eve resolution easily gets broken six weeks after its made. (Yes, that is the industry statistic for more than half of all the people who join a gym in January!) So it helps to anticipate (there's that ever-so-important concept again) what is next on the horizon. Constantly ask yourself and your clients, "What do you want next?" The benefit of keeping close contact with your customers is their feedback!

When you are an entrepreneur interested in keeping ahead of the curve, the seemingly mundane starts to matter. At Retro Fitness, we don't want any customer to complain about a dusty dumbbell or a sweaty screen on the treadmill. We always put ourselves in our customers' shoes. We think like the customer who has never entered a gym—the one who is intimidated. We talk to our customers and listen to them daily as we roam around the floor. We don't risk losing even one customer to a dust bunny in the corner under a machine, or to the discomfort of having to search out the ten-pound dumbbell that was misplaced in a rack of hundred-pounders. We want all Retro Fitness customers to get fit, and to feel like they fit in.

That is why our Retro Fitness employees always say hello and goodbye to members. Our exit door signs read, "See You Tomorrow," because we believe in our customers' commitment to us and to their own goals. We remind them to come back and visit again not just frequently, but soon.

> **Think about some ways your customers might be able to create social bonds among not just your staff, but one another. I assure you the benefits from this will be worth the invested time and capital.**

We engage members at the fitness level, as well as the social level. Your business should feel to locals like their local bar—you want to go where everybody knows your name. I call it the "Cheers" effect—everybody knew Norm when he walked in the door! Even if we don't have a twenty-minute conversation with every customer who comes in, we have greeted them. Your employee's smile and gesture might be the nicest interaction they had all day, or maybe all week! We might chat them up at the juice bar, or introduce them to other members.

Bonds form between the 5:00 a.m. members, as well as among the 5:00 p.m. crowd. Bonds create retention; they generate commitment. And ultimately, this results in members meeting their fitness goals, and in us meeting our business goals. Think about some ways your customers might be able to create social bonds among not just your staff, but one another. I assure you the benefits from this will be worth the invested time and capital.

People may come in with friends or they may come in alone, but more often than not, they want to be social on some level. Different subsets of customers will have different habits and routines. It's part of human behavior, and it's a need we continuously foster at Retro Fitness. We've got members who met at our juice bar and have since gotten married! How's that for grand slamming social engagement?

People have a need to socialize. The human body needs socialization as much as it needs a certain balance of vitamins, minerals, and so on. Your company, product, or service needs to somehow fulfill that need if you want long-term success. People often hear me say ,"The general population NEEDS Retro Fitness whether they know it yet or not!" We try to stamp ourselves in our customers' DNA. You brush your teeth and leave your house with your cell phone without even thinking about it—these acts are automatic, and so should your workout at Retro Fitness be.

We believe your gym time is your time—the gym is truly one of the only remaining places in our culture where you can take time out *just for you, for your wellbeing*. We train this mentality into our team members and franchisees at Retro University. We need our team to truly believe that each member should highly value the time he or she spends with us.

The "RU" is the starting point for our people to learn how best to serve members, and to begin to learn what they need now and what they will need in the future. We do both in-house and on-site training, and once we have teams in place, an auditor regularly checks in on them. We have someone from one of my offices walk around with an iPad that contains a hundred-point checklist of the "key" touch points in our gyms. This visit is usually unannounced, so that we can see the business running in its normal course. If anything is found lacking, or if any employees are found slacking, we take a look first at where someone might make a better fit. We consider strengths and weaknesses and make personnel change recommendations as well as operational change recommendations, if and when necessary.

Our franchisees don't fear this visit; on the contrary, they love it because they value their businesses and want them to be the best they can be. Our employee education is ongoing and thorough—our employees are a source of inspiration to members and a source of pride to management teams. They are usually the first point of contact with my brand. They must be as committed to Retro Fitness as I am if they want to work for

> **You can never stop improving in business. You can never rest on yesterday's success. Being an entrepreneur is about continual growth.**

my company—they must engage with the brand and care about it as much as the owners do. They must "drink the Kool-Aid," as I like to put it.

You can never stop improving in business. You can never rest on yesterday's success. Being an entrepreneur is about continual growth.

One company that does this on an amazing level is Disney. One of Disney's latest apps allows you to make reservations at restaurants around the resort and connect with other members of your party to share reservation information. The "Fast Pass" option expedites your wait in lines for rides, and links with a wristband that allows you to do everything from opening your hotel room door to purchasing a hot dog or Mickey Mouse ears. You don't even need your wallet at Disney anymore! I find that I now spend money more easily there, but also more happily.

I'm thrilled to go to Disney and I'm thrilled to conveniently spend my money there. The employee training program at Disney University and Disney Institute is a huge part of what makes Disney theme parks such an over-the-top bonding experience for everyone. Because each employee is considered a Cast Member, the culture of "it's all about the show" reaches directly down to the customer.

Disney thinks so far ahead on the service level that they have begun to scent the lobbies of their higher-end on-property resorts, hitting our most primal senses and creating a fantastic subconscious anchor. When I learned about this, I hired the same company to create a scent program for all of my gyms. Why not turn the gym experience into an even more enticing and invigorating one? Our members love the difference, whether they realize exactly what that difference is or not. Now, hopefully, when they leave their workout, they can avoid the drive-through window of the fast-food joint that is pumping out the scent of french fries!

The point is, taking a page out of a winner's successful playbook is always a good idea. You might want to write that one down in your notepad! Please tell me you have a notepad at your side any time you're reading a book.

TAKEAWAY

- The key to success is to think ahead, to anticipate the public's needs and desires, to give them something they didn't even realize they wanted. *What do **you** want that no one is making or doing?*

CHAPTER THREE

Resourcefulness: How You Get Better as an Entrepreneur... Quickly

I MENTIONED it earlier, and it's worth stating again: If your family practitioner told you that you were gravely ill or at risk for a certain disease, you would immediately go for a second opinion, see a specialist, research all you could online, and do whatever you could do every single day to remedy the situation. Similarly, if your business took a hit—a new competitor set up shop two blocks down, or the economy hit the skids (again)—you would have to rally. You would gather your team (or if you don't have a team, you'd do it alone), brainstorm, and investigate all available resources. Learning to gather the needed resources for the given task at hand is the first practical principle of "resourcefulness," but is just the beginning.

Whether you run a restaurant, a small retail clothing store, or a gym—any business—as an entrepreneur you need to know the importance of "the check up from the neck up." You know I'm not talking about that annual visit to your primary physician. I'm talking about the unique challenge that, as an entrepreneur, you have to contend with at times, and that is sometimes your own worst enemy—yourself.

You need to be very critical of your own behavior and performance—and OFTEN. I recently attended a seminar led by a very well respected speaker/author, and he said something that truly resonated with me. He said, "If you want to locate *the source of the chokehold in most businesses*, you have to look no further than the business owners themselves."

> **Check yourself before you wreck yourself may sound retro to some ears, but it's a timeless and solid piece of advice.**

Realize that you can be your business's biggest obstacle—your thinking, your habits, your inflexible opinions about how things should be, your work ethic, your lack of knowledge— any of these factors, if you aren't aware of them, can inhibit your progress. *Check yourself before you wreck yourself* may sound retro to some ears, but it's a timeless and solid piece of advice.

How you perceive challenges, stay focused, and beat the mental and physical exhaustion or self-defeat out of your own mind is crucial. When that competition does come around and you hear people talking about checking it out, you'd better hope you've already figured out a plan that will allow you to adapt. Being a business owner never gets easier: rent never goes down, labor costs always go up, and word-of-mouth now moves at the speed of lightning thanks to the Internet. Owning a business means you can never slow down. This isn't me just coming to you as the Retro Fitness guy: this is me as an entrepreneur and small-business owner telling you that you can save yourself a lot of headache if, from Day One—even when *you* are the new kid on the block—you stay agile and well prepared.

Look, we all are aging, but we know there are actions we can take to slow that process down. The same is true in business: If we stay healthy and relevant, we can stay in the game.

Ichak Adizes covers this topic in his wise and wonderful book, *Corporate Lifecycles*, with the major takeaway being the idea of *keeping* yourself at the "Peak" stage of your business cycle. Getting to the top is much easier than *staying* at the top, and I speak from experience. You will see a whole new set of challenges once you and your business actually become successful. The key is to look at your new problems as "good problems." Hey, it means you've gotten somewhere! But again, maintaining your business at its peak stage will take much *more* resourcefulness.

You must continue to improve upon the successes you have had, and learn from the mistakes you have made so you don't repeat them. You would be surprised how many businesses repeat stupid mistakes and expect different results. There is no excuse for that kind of ignorance or laziness. We all know the

> **You must continue to improve upon the successes you have had, and learn from the mistakes you have made so you don't repeat them.**
>
> ———
>
> **Fix your mistakes, avoid repeating them, and move on.**

saying: "You can't expect to repeat the same process and get a different outcome." Fix your mistakes, avoid repeating them, and move on.

When you feel that first dip in business—and all businesses do shake some after initial liftoff—are you ready to try something new? Have you been thinking outside the box during the flush times, so that in rough times you can continue to move forward?

If you're not paying attention, success can lull you to sleep. Every day I see people resting on their laurels, on the successful path they forged yesterday, with no regard for tomorrow's journey. I see owners start to do well—cash flow is positive—and they believe they are winning the game. The problem is, while you may think you are unstoppable and that nobody can take an ounce of market share or a single customer from you, as time goes on your product gets old, your equipment doesn't work as well, and your menu becomes boring to some of your customers. When change is in order and you aren't at the Peak stage of your business, you will find it hard to move quickly, and even harder to recover.

If the competition has pulled away some of your clients, can you afford to set an employee out on the sidewalk wearing a sign offering a 2-for-1 special or some other type of aggressive promotion? You have to *think Darwinian*, in the good and the bad times. Mix things up—combine forces with another local business or up your advertising strategy or mail out a coupon that nobody can refuse. If you planned for your first (or second) inevitable rough patch, then you were smart enough to put some cash away when times were good. Walking through a rainstorm is much more palatable when you are prepared with an umbrella. Do you have your business umbrella?

You know that the rewards of running your own business are immeasurable. You are building your own empire, increasing your cash flow, hopefully taking advantage of certain tax benefits, and ultimately building a lifetime of total freedom for yourself. Entrepreneurs are passionate and forward-thinking by nature, and though those sixteen-hour days can sometimes wear you down, there is nothing like the adrenalin rush of risking it all to keep a business alive and thriving. Taking the initiative and giving directions is simply part of who the entrepreneur is, and with that power and responsibility, there is no such thing as leaving work on the desk, closing the office door, and shutting off the constant internal engine.

Being resourceful is crucial in all stages of entrepreneurship—in fact, resourcefulness is what helps a high percentage of entrepreneurs start their own businesses in the first place. Most of us have gone to banks and to family members, business plan in hand, and tried to borrow the money to fund our dreams. "I want this and I can do this," we say. "What are my lending options?" We eat up periodicals on entrepreneurship and attend seminars, sometimes sifting through ninety pounds of junk to find a one-ounce golden nugget—but we find it.

NETWORKING IS the entrepreneur's middle name. If you are threatened by other people's success, you probably aren't a true entrepreneur, and it may be tough for you to hack it over the long term. Entrepreneurs draw and are drawn to successful people in their own fields. Anthony Robbins refers to this as "the power of proximity," and I am a subscriber to that theory.

You should be constantly seeking out the stories of business people, investors, attorneys, accountants, and creative types.

> **Networking is the entrepreneur's middle name.**
>
> ———
>
> **Entrepreneurs draw and are drawn to successful people in their own fields.**

Why would you spend your valuable lunch hour alone behind your desk or with anyone who doesn't educate you in some way about how to run your business better? Entrepreneurs seek enlightenment—it helps with that "check up from the neck up." It's good to have a benchmark to measure yourself and your business against. The key is to measure consistently as you grow, and to move your benchmarks when needed.

Meeting other experts is all part of building your resources, and so the more experts you come into contact with, the more resourceful you'll be when the time calls for it. You want to franchise your business? Start by asking yourself, "Who has done this successfully?" One fast track to success is finding those who have done what you want to do, and mimicking their patterns. Just make sure you are observing and picking up the relevant and right patterns.

What kinds of questions can you ask that will save you time and money in the future? I asked thousands of questions before the launching of Retro Fitness, and the number one thing I consistently heard was: Stick to your marketing and advertising budget, no matter what. I repeat what was repeated to me time and time again: Do not waver on your marketing and advertising budget, even in tough times. Stay the course.

Another piece of expert advice I received that was more specific to the service industry—my industry—was keep the bathrooms clean and hire a friendly staff.

We discussed in previous chapters the importance of doing our best in a "touch environment" to keep our equipment clean and our shelves tidy. And it cannot be stated often enough: Having someone at the first point of contact who knows how to make patrons feel great when entering and exiting your business is crucial. This may sound simple, but you will be surprised how quickly you will forget about this after you get started and the first round of employees leaves to go back to college.

We have talked some about knowing your employees and understanding their strengths and weaknesses. There are ways to find the perfect roles for each and every personality type. But of course, before you can build your great empire, it is critical that *you know yourself* too. Most entrepreneurs have fairly extroverted personalities and can create a rapport easily. Handling people is the entrepreneur's specialty. You need to maximize your skill set, and train those who show the same potential.

Remember too, that an impressive education or a sterling resume is not always the key to being successful at what you do. Many of the world's most successful innovators and entrepreneurs never started or finished college. I fall into the college dropout category myself, as I tell every reporter who interviews me, from *Forbes* to *Entreprenuer* magazine.

No textbook will ever teach you what to do when the first crazy person walks into your place of business and starts shouting obscenities at your front-end cashier! "Learning by doing" will be your mantra when you start out running your own show. Your bookkeeper quits with only a day's notice; your top salesperson is going to work for the competition; the employee who holds the office together with her vivacious personality is getting divorced and moving across the country—these are just a few examples of the entrepreneur's most common war stories.

Resourceful individuals and companies always have a backup plan, and your employees have to know what that plan is—money and valuable customers can be lost if there is no plan, or if the original plan falls apart. When you stay in a hotel, there's a hotel-exit strategy just in case of fire on the back of your door. "Just in case" is the second mantra of the entrepreneur.

> **Always go in with the best intentions, but prepare for the worst outcome, and you will have a better shot at success.**

This doesn't mean we are all negative thinkers; it means we are intelligent and prepared. Always go in with the best intentions, but prepare for the worst outcome, and you will have a better shot at success.

I opened a brand-new RetroFitness in a great location. All the new equipment had arrived and been set up. Members were flocking in. "So far, so great!" everyone was saying. And then the landlord contacted us and said he wanted to do some roof work. "Okay," we said, "Whatever the building needs."

The roofers started their work on a Friday, on a beautiful summer evening, and the landlord's contractor decided he'd leave the roof open so the inspector could quickly stop in and inspect the work on Monday morning. But an unexpected thunderstorm hit the region that weekend. It rained like cats and dogs all night long, and there was nothing we could do immediately, as we were closed for the day.

The following morning when we arrived, we put into action our standard "Hazard Plan." We have a list of local contractors, including the ones who worked on our original construction, as they know the ins and outs of the building.

We started a "phone chain," systematically calling all the necessary resources we would need to get back on track as fast as possible. We called everyone from flood restoration companies to cleaning companies to electricians. Looking at the damage the rain had caused, nobody ever would have guessed that we would have that gym up and running within sixteen hours—but we did. I even had the gym painted overnight so it looked perfect the next opening morning.

The point is, when disaster hits—your top sales associate leaves two days prior to a crucial meeting, or a sprinkler system blows overnight in your store (yes, this happened to me as well, but I'll save that story for another book!)—*how* you handle it matters most. You can't spend one minute, let alone a full day, crying or throwing a fit over lost equipment or materials. You've got five seconds to cry, and the rest of the hour to put your plan into action. Let me repeat: How you handle challenges can mean the difference between life or death for your business. You must embrace resourcefulness.

> **How you handle challenges can mean the difference between life or death for your business.**

I have been resourceful since childhood. My mother passed away when I was just 16, leaving behind my father, my brother, and me. Prior to Mom's passing, we had never had to do laundry, cook, or clean—she always happily handled those tasks. We had to adapt quickly. Losing my mother was awful, but I like to look at the event in as positive a light as I can. Learning to live without her shaped my thinking, and that was a gift that kept on giving—I use the same strategies today.

TAKEAWAY

- Challenges, setbacks, and mistakes are inevitable in business and in life, and one can succeed only by keeping a level head and being resourceful in dealing with these obstacles.
  How well do you handle stress? How could you improve?

CHAPTER FOUR

Either You're an Entrepreneur Today, or You Will Be

IT'S NO secret that the economy has suffered in the past few years—the U.S. job market has been annihilated. So many of the statistics we read are fluff—jobs appear to be on the rise, but what kind of jobs? Not the kind most people can survive on. Statistics these days seem to reflect whatever side of the political agenda someone is on, without really stating the bottom line, which is this: now more than ever, when it comes to your career, you need to take charge of your own destiny. Nothing is guaranteed, not even a pension—just ask the folks who tried to retire in 2008!

People from all economic classes and all job fields have felt the crunch—maybe your company downsized and your hours were reduced; maybe your position was cut altogether. Maybe you haven't seen a salary increase in over a decade and have had to take on a second job to pay off your refinanced mortgage. There are many factors to take into account when we discuss the real truth about today's job market.

Forget about the politics or the rhetoric you see on the business news channels. I am here to tell you how it really is, as a guy who is in the trenches with my fellow business owners and franchisees day in and day out. Technology is miraculous, but it is forcing people out of work. It's great if you're a business owner and four kiosks can take the place of three humans at the checkout, but it's not so great if you're the employee. Being part of a thriving global economy has its advantages, of course, but watching our jobs being moved overseas is not one of them. The truth is, everywhere across our country, people young and old are being made redundant, and some young people can't even find jobs worthy of their education. It's almost impossible to turn on the news and not hear about how this issue is affecting everyone at some level.

Nobody is immune to the realities of the U.S. job market. It makes sense now more than ever to want to take control of your own destiny. People who grasp entrepreneurship sooner rather than later are ahead of the game. Why wait for another economic crisis to hit? Why not plan for tomorrow, with the understanding that no matter what your position is today, there are no guarantees anymore? If you are not running your own game—if you do not own your own business—you truly have no control over your financial future.

I know the cold, hard facts may sting a bit, but I'm not here to sugarcoat anything. I'm writing this book to help direct you to the life you deserve.

When you take over the steering wheel of your future, you are the driving force, and you alone are in charge of your security. For some, that's a frightening notion; some people prefer to rely on the government or the company. The problem of course is that even if you are Big XYZ Company's rainmaker today, tomorrow Big XYZ could sell his business to his son, and that son could decide he wants to bring in his college buddy to do your job—so it's "Adios!" to you.

Even if you have never considered yourself an entrepreneur, know this—all you need to make the transformation are two key ingredients—passion and drive. Some of you already have the passion and drive in you and have perhaps been running a side business alongside your regular job. Or you've opened a business and are thinking of expanding to another. Wherever you are on the path toward entrepreneurship, you are on the path—and this is all that matters. If you are still holding this book in your hands, at this point you have recognized that you have a great idea and have conquered whatever fears you might have, including, "What if this idea doesn't pan out?" You have understood your fears, managed them, and removed them from the playing field.

When your mind is set, you understand that success leads to further success. Your first accomplishment may have been simply conquering fear of failure. Great! Then you set yourself out on the path and began to talk to those experts in entrepreneurship who surround you. Entrepreneurs are everywhere, and they are the smart ones. They are the ones who realize that our nation was built upon a very strong principle of self-sufficiency, and that it was time for self-sufficiency to rise again. Entrepreneurs know they need to reach out to others, study hard, learn constantly, and get back into the game immediately after taking a fall.

People with the entrepreneurial spirit know they are not experts at all tasks in business—this is, indeed, one of the strengths of the entrepreneur. You figure out what you are good at; you come up with a list of good traits, and then you do the exact same exercise for things you are *not* good at handling. You may find that the list of good traits is only one page long, and the list of bad traits is four pages long. So be it. Now you know exactly the kind of people you need to hire to support you and your goals. You know what kind of expertise you must seek out.

Now grab a pen and turn to the lined pages in the back of this book, and make your list of business skills and traits you have … and a list of those you don't have. The former list contains all the things you'll do, the latter tells you what tasks you'll need to delegate to someone better qualified. Take however long you need—ten minutes or ten hours. Don't be afraid to be self-congratulatory or self-critical. What's most important is that you do this simple exercise. Regardless of what stage you are at in the business life cycle, breaking down and reviewing your skills can be extremely helpful, and it will allow you to identify sooner who is going to do what.

Amen to the "check-up from the neck-up" evaluation.

I believe an entrepreneur has to have an open and wild imagination in business. In meetings, I'll throw twenty new ideas out on the table. Three of those ideas might be usable, so we get to work on those as soon as possible (there you have that *take action* concept again). And I can sell; I am always selling. Selling is one of the more important skill sets for a new business owner. I know some of you reading this are thinking *sell*, *salesperson*, and *sales pitch* are dirty words, but you have to get over that misconception quickly.

When you have an awesome product, you are doing a disservice to the world by not being able to communicate

> When you have an awesome product, you are doing a disservice to the world by not being able to communicate how amazing it is. Think of sales as simply educating people, through a friendly and honest conversation, about how awesome your product is.

Always be on! how amazing it is. Think of sales as simply educating people, through a friendly and honest conversation, about how awesome your product is. Whether you want to sell a pencil eraser or a Rolls Royce, show you believe in your product. Smile about it, be honest about it, believe in it, and don't stop talking about it. Recently I went into a store to buy a drone to use for taking aerial views of potential new locations for Retro Fitness. I came out of the store having sold a half-dozen memberships to customers in the shop, and I had even discussed starting a franchise with the store owner. Always be on!

The point is, being a successful entrepreneur does not require rocket science or some deep magic formula. It's not true that money attracts money; a good salesperson and a smile attract money. So know that even if you are shy, you can learn a few angles. If you aren't the type to strike up conversations wherever you go, practice on the friends and family you already have, and on their friends. Roleplaying is a lost art these days, and that's a shame. You need to get comfortable talking with strangers as if you've known each other since childhood. Establishing a rapport quickly with a potential client, investor, or prospect could be the key that opens new doors for you and your business.

There are few business schools that teach entrepreneurial skills, because entrepreneurship is so much about *spirit*.

Schools will teach you the things your brain needs to absorb and regurgitate, but they can't teach you about having passion or heart. Many of us can relate to the athlete who was smaller, slower, and not as nimble as some of his competitors, but because he had heart, he was driven to give it his all and never quit—until he triumphed.

Everyone has a passion, but traditionally we aren't conditioned to look for it, understand it, or name it. Even if we do discover it, we aren't trained to *use it*. Most MBA programs teach people how to climb the corporate ladder. Success is measured in all the same terms and by the same parameters. True entrepreneurs are the square pegs that will not fit into the round holes.

Entrepreneurs *are* their businesses—there are no training wheels here. Once you discover that freewheeling spirit in yourself, you realize you are stepping into territory where there are no rules except for the ones you create for yourself.

Entrepreneurs *are* their businesses—there are no training wheels here. Once you discover that freewheeling spirit in yourself, you realize you are stepping into territory where there are no rules except for the ones you create for yourself. And so you must create them. This may sound pretty good at first, but when you realize how much self discipline it takes to create those rules, you recognize it for the undertaking it is. Let that soak in for a moment or two.

Success comes to those who know their strengths. Once you understand what you are good at, and what you'll need help with, you can move forward with that understanding and create goals. You list your top goals, set them on a timeline, and resolve to adjust along the way as you and your goals transform. Later on I will discuss goal-setting strategies and ideas.

At first, in the early days of running your own show, you may work ridiculous hours—your life may be your work. But there will be a payoff.

In business, if you are not growing you are receding. There is no such thing as stillness. Business is constantly moving—in which direction is up to you.

As you begin to run your business—and experience failure and success—you will learn everything you need to know, from how to run your lighting system at maximum efficiency to scheduling, IT needs, and emergency preparedness. As you learn, you should itemize and document every practice and procedure. The document you eventually end up with will become your operations manual—your company Bible—and you'll use it to train others, and eventually to hire the person who will take over some of your responsibilities so that you can go out and drum up more business and grow your company. In business, if you are not growing you are receding. There is no such thing as stillness. Business is constantly moving—in which direction is up to you.

You are an entrepreneur, in part, because you do not want to spend all your time in the trenches, being moved around at somebody else's whim. You want the freedom to enjoy your family and friends. By systematizing your duties you can begin to have that freedom. Whenever I meet with new franchisees, often one of the first questions I hear is, "But how long will I have to work the eighty-hour workweek?" My answer: "The system you will be learning was designed by someone just like you—someone who figured out how to organize and systemize his business because he wants his children to grow up knowing who he is. I wrote the book here, folks. My life goals are the same as yours."

Freedom is what entrepreneurship is all about. In order to gain that freedom you have to let go of your fear of failure, learn your strengths and weaknesses, systematize your business, hire and train the right people, and learn to let go again. Trust that once you have built that foundation, which will require lots of heavy lifting at the start, you will eventually be able to spend more time away from the business, doing the $10 million work instead of the $10 per hour work, or taking family time. You can take three-day weekends if you want to.

Delegating is not always easy for the entrepreneur—not for the beginner entrepreneur, and not for the established one either. Most entrepreneurs give directions by saying, "Move out of the way, I'll do it myself." But learning to keep your Alpha mode in check will be the best thing you've ever done for yourself. After setting up your business systems, build that foundation, hand over one of the keys to someone else, get to your kid's soccer game on time, and breathe deeply. Be happy, and humble enough to understand that someone can now run your thriving business without you hovering over their shoulders eighty hours a week. Let go—this is freedom.

TAKEAWAYS

- Today's economy is very unstable, and true job security is hard to come by except through entrepreneurship.
- It is important to know what you're good at and what you're not, and to be willing to delegate to others any tasks for which you are not well suited. *What are you good at? What are you **not** so good at?*

CHAPTER FIVE

Raising a Fortune:
Why Doesn't Anybody Want
to Talk About Money?

HUNDREDS OF books have been written about money—how to make it, save it, invest and reinvest it, shelter it, and so on. And still the average person has a tough time dealing with money because they don't understand real-world economics. Most people don't understand the benefit of choosing debt as leverage to become wealthy. Most people hear the word "debt" and think about bad debt—they think of the horror stories from 2008, or about folks with a dozen credit cards. And while it is true that some of the statistics on Americans and debt are alarming (for example: "On average, each household with a credit card carries more than $15,000 in credit card debt," and "the total U.S. consumer debt is at $11.4 trillion"[1]), entrepreneurs and the wealthy know that the right kind of debt is good.

---

1 http://www.debt.org/faqs/americans-in-debt/

> **Good debt produces income. It produces cash flow. When we talk about going into good debt on a business, it all comes down to understanding cash flow.**

Good debt produces income. It produces cash flow. When we talk about going into good debt on a business, it all comes down to understanding cash flow. Many people are confused when they get started: "OK, I am going to start a business. So I have to have all the start-up money, right?" No. Some banks will lend you money if you have a solid business plan, a healthy credit history, and some down payment money. Work experience in your business segment is beneficial, as well. It may take a few attempts at first, but don't give up. Just think about how many doors Walt Disney had to knock on before someone gave him the "yes" he was seeking. Over three hundred bankers rejected Walt Disney's theme park business proposal—a couple of mice, a duck, and what? What if Disney had quit after the three-hundredth "no"?

Eventually, as you become a more sophisticated business operator and show that you are good at what you do, banks will lend you money simply because you have a track record and have proved yourself. Sure, your first business may require a bit more blood, sweat, and tears because you haven't yet made a name for yourself. But once you prove yourself, and once you move on to your second and third business, you will have realized the value of good debt—you will have begun to understand how more debt can in fact make you more money.

The right kind of debt can help produce positive cash flow. The wrong kind of debt—say you buy a house with a mortgage that is above your means—produces negative cash flow. If you take on a million-dollar mortgage to buy your house, you own a liability; but if you take a million-dollar mortgage out on a business that has cash flow, and you pay down that debt from that cash flow—you own an asset. You have invested in something smart that hopefully continues to appreciate.

Anyone can be a paper investor. Paper investors invest in stocks and bonds and 401(k) plans, but they don't get involved in anything else because it all seems so complicated. The truth is, investing in a business can be much more lucrative than investing in "paper," and it can also give you a lot more control of your money. If you invest in Apple, you can't pick up the phone and call the company president if you disagree with how the company is operating. But when you are investing in your own business, you are in direct contact with all decision makers. This gives you much more control over your investment.

If you are utilizing debt on a business that has cash flow, or using debt to structure a deal that will allow you to have multiple opportunities, you are in control of your money— and more important, of your life. Let's say you have a hundred thousand dollars and you want to open a lemonade stand. You can spend all that money to build one lemonade stand on the best corner in your city, or you can take that hundred thousand dollars, go to the bank and get three hundred thousand dollars, and buy three lemonade stands.

By opening three lemonade stands instead of one, you have diversified your assets and bought yourself some security—if one lemonade stand goes bad, and you've only got the one, you're in big trouble. But if you've got three and one goes bad, the other two can absorb the loss and counter the negative cash flow.

There is a learning curve required to understand how to use debt to your benefit, and a lot of business owners don't realize it, especially in the early going. They say, "Uh oh, I want to open this business, but it costs X and I need to spend a lot of time and effort to raise X by myself." The truth is, you don't. You can go to the bank as discussed earlier, or you can bring on investing partners—what it all comes back to is the entrepreneurial skill of selling.

One of the greatest things I was able to do as a young entrepreneur was to sell not only my product, but to also myself. If you show a bank or a prospective business partner that you are a diligent, hardworking, consistent, and successful planner, you will get results; they will throw money at you. If you believe in yourself and in your product, believe me, people will invest in you and your business. But you MUST get results. Investors want to know what success you have already had in your field.

> **If you show a bank or a prospective business partner that you are a diligent, hardworking, consistent, and successful planner, you will get results; they will throw money at you.**

Selling yourself may seem difficult at first for some, but with practice it will become second nature. Keep in mind: The best business plan is nothing without a personality delivering it. You may have the best idea since sliced bread, and you may present the best-written business plan a team of investors has ever read, but if you have the personality of a doorknob, nobody will give you a nickel—because at the

> **The best business plan is nothing without a personality delivering it.**

end of the day, people do business with people. That is why a lot of business is done in restaurants and on golf courses. People want to *like* you and your business, because they are considering both as potential long-term, mutually beneficial relationships.

Communication skills cannot be overlooked when it comes to running a successful business and making more money.

Share your passion—sell it. I can't stress enough the importance of good communication skills. Communication skills cannot be overlooked when it comes to running a successful business and making more money. It pays—literally— to be able to sit down with someone, establish a rapport, and have an educated conversation at their level regardless. If you aren't a born communicator, you can learn how to be one when necessary. There are countless resources for improving communication skills, and most can be found at your local bookstore.

Consider yourself your own diverse portfolio. Treat yourself like a mutual fund. If you have X dollars, invest in things you can control. Educate yourself about all the cash benefits of owning a business. The government gives small business owners incentives for a reason. They want you to open businesses, because if you create more jobs, they will collect more taxes.

There are basic tax perks for you as a business owner, too. When you sell a paper stock, odds are you are going to pay a significant tax, but when you take something such as dividend income out of your business, you are taxed at a much lower rate. Of course, you will want a team of tax and legal professionals working with you in order to maximize the opportunities available—but realize that everything down to the car you use for business and the meals you eat with prospective investors and clients are all tax-deductible, putting money right back in your pocket.

When the cash does start to flow, knowing what to do with that money can seem difficult at first, but it's simple, really: Treat your business like a person, and give it its own checking and savings account. When you start making money in your business, you don't want to make the mistake of withdrawing all of it and putting it in your pocket. Treat your business as an individual that has its own savings account for rainy days.

> **Don't go out spending money on fancy cars and shoes until you have a pre-determined amount of rainy-day money in your business's savings account.**

If I make $5 today, I do not take out $4.99 and leave my business with a penny. Always have a threshold number that needs to stay in the bank—in the savings account of the business—before you pocket even one dollar. Exercise discipline, and as soon as there is positive cash flow, stop and do your math: If it costs $20,000 a month to run your business, and the business is making $25,000 a month (therefore, netting $5,000, before you take any of that profit), check to ensure at minimum that you have at least two to three-months' worth of capital saved. Take nothing until you have filled that well—the savings account—with what you need. Don't go out spending money on fancy cars and shoes until you have a pre-determined amount of rainy-day money in your business's savings account.

It is a challenge to subvert the debt-ridden consumer culture we are part of, but the recession was a big wake-up call for many. Owning a successful business and leveraging debt to your advantage takes common sense, patience, and discipline. But remember your ultimate goal: true control over your own money and freedom. It will come. Once you have saved your pre-determined two or three months' dollar amount—your $60,000 on your $20,000-a-month business—then the next dollar you make is yours. The good news is, your business is profitable.

Now your business is performing well and you get to take your share of the profit—say it's an additional $5,000 a month. You can put it in your personal savings account or use it for whatever you want. What I recommend, as you may have guessed, is that you invest in another business.

> Owning a successful business and leveraging debt to your advantage takes common sense, patience, and discipline. But remember your ultimate goal: true control over your own money and freedom. It will come.

Think about what I said earlier about your initial trip to the bank, and think about subsequent trips to that bank: Now that you have proved you can make money with their money, the bank says, "Wow. This person really knows what they're doing. They've got cash flow in their business and positive equity in the bank. They're a great investment. Let's lend them more money!"

You have come a long way. You raised the money to start your first business, and you socked X amount away for a rainy day, and you have also pocketed some profit. Maybe you are on your second or third business now. And now, inevitably, the rainy day does come—it could be a competitor or a recession, but it hits. Something will happen that will affect your normally consistent cash flow, no matter what stage of entrepreneurship you are on. But guess what—you won't be biting your nails and staying up all night like some other guys will be, because of your diligent savings. You won't have to worry as much as the other guys because you have the funds to maintain the health of your business, and to keep your product quality high. You can continue to advertise and do the necessary marketing, never burying your head in the sand. The savings account methodology for business has allowed you to avoid added stress, and this allows for much better decision making as you navigate the troubled waters ahead.

When the days are good, you have got to save money because there will come a time—a short-lived one we hope— when you are going to have to fight a little harder than you are today. That's business. But if you keep a Darwinian mindset—you have to be the last man standing—you will survive the lean times.

Invest in your decisions and in yourself, and always continue to educate yourself. Attend seminars, read books, and learn about good debt and how to leverage it. Realize you will never be able to call Warren Buffet and ask him why a certain stock changed—you have zero control over what happens to your portfolio if you have all paper assets. But you can always control what happens in your business.

Don't buy into the standard advice of so many financial advisors, which is to prepare for being poorer when you retire. They will tell you to invest today with pre-tax dollars in a 401(k) or an SEP-type investment plan, and pay taxes later when you take the earnings out because when you retire you will be in a lower tax bracket. That's crazy thinking! If you are a real entrepreneur, you believe you are going to continue to grow your business along with your cash and net worth. You'd better be dreaming of retiring in *the highest tax bracket*, because you'll have so much income.

You need to make a choice now about how you want to run your life, make your money, and retire. As Stephen Covey says, "Begin with the End in mind." I know people who work into their seventies because they have to, because they had no plan. I am here to tell you that you need to start being smarter about how you invest the hard-earned money you earn. Owning a business is smart. Look at where the wealthiest invest, and then learn what they learned.

Don't just throw your hands up in the air and say, "It's too complicated, I'll just listen to the advice of some advisor," when that advisor is probably is making a lot less money than you! Do you know why they call them "brokers?" Because they are "broker" than you! Seriously though, do you really want or plan to live a more miserly life in retirement, when you worked so hard all these years? Why not go out with a solid gold walker? Why not provide the best for yourself and your family, starting today and for as long as you can?

We are talking about real dollars and real life in this chapter. Your money is worth less every day, as the government keeps printing more of it. If you don't have a sense of urgency while this book is in your hands, shame on you! If you haven't figured out a way to get started running and controlling your own show, act now, before it is too late.

TAKEAWAYS

- If you know how to use it, debt can actually be a useful tool for making money.
- Once you have some initial success, banks will be much more willing to lend you money, but only if you are able to sell yourself well.
- Always have at least two to three-months' worth of capital saved in order to carry your business through the inevitable lean times.

Chapter Six

Marketing: If You Spend the Minimum, Expect the Minimum

IN THE previous chapter, we discussed everybody's favorite topic: making money. The bottom line is—and it bears repeating in this chapter—you have to spend money to make money. Money has to flow out to flow back in. And although this concept is difficult to understand for people who are new to business, there is a formula to follow, and it works.

When you are in business, you are going to read a million books, articles, blogs, and blurbs about marketing. Retro Fitness could certainly write our own (and in fact, we have). All franchises have a formula; for instance, Retro Fitness has a minimum you must spend in marketing and advertising monthly—it is required—otherwise we will default you. You read that right: we will actually default a franchisee who does not spend the minimum on marketing and advertising, because we understand how important it is.

When you talk about your business's money, it is imperative that you have a line item in the budget for marketing. That line item should not be a fixed number, for example, our Retro Fitness minimum is the baseline, but it adjusts to a percentage calculated on how much the business grows. This means your baseline percentage for marketing and advertising should start at a minimum, but then be tied to a growing number. The minimum might be $1,000 a month or $25,000 a month—either way, a good rule of thumb is to allot at least five to ten percent of your gross revenue to your marketing budget.

Five percent is the absolute minimum, but ten is much more effective. Now some might say, "Whoa, what about when I start making $100,000 a month? Am I still supposed to spend ten percent—$10,000 a month—on marketing?" I tell people, "Stop thinking so far ahead. Yes, let's hope you start making $100,000 a month, and let's review new ranges for marketing if and when that time comes."

The point is, all too often, marketing is the first thing that gets cut from the budget and the last thing that gets added—and either way is bad business. Too many new business owners make the mistake of cutting their marketing budget once things get tight, or their marketing budget is the last thing they add when starting out. Most people don't realize it should be the reverse: money for marketing and advertising has to be the last thing that gets cut when times are tough, and the first thing that gets added when you are starting out.

Many people decide to take the leap into entrepreneurship, urged on by thoughts of freedom, control, and making money. But prior to attaining the dream, understanding why, how, and what to spend is crucial.

...money for marketing and advertising has to be the last thing that gets cut when times are tough, and the first thing that gets added when you are starting out.

What to spend does not have to be complicated— you have to set parameters that have meaning. When you are creating a business plan, start with a pro forma or a spreadsheet that lines up for you: I'm expecting to have sales of X (Income), I'm expecting to spend Y (Expenses), and in the bottom right corner, I'm going to make Z (Net Profit … hopefully). When you draw up your business plan, you have to know what all expenses should be if that plan is to be a useful tool.

Once you have established your minimum number, you cannot retract it—ever. Marketing is a twelve-month-a-year com-

There is no such thing as a "season" for marketing...

mitment. There is no such thing as a "season" for marketing, even if you run a summertime tourist business along the shore, or a ski resort business in the mountains. Whether you are selling boogie boards or snowboards, you need to be in front of customers twelve months a year because you need to stay relevant and on their minds.

Out of sight is out of mind in the world of business, and you become irrelevant the moment you stop being seen. Your competition will strike—whether they are in your neighborhood, in your market, or online—if you fade out of sight for even just one month of the year. If you are not visible and your competitor is, it will be that much harder for you to regain access to your customers' hearts and minds. In fact, it won't just be hard; it may be impossible.

You don't feed your dog half the year. You don't shower only half the week. Being seen year-round is that important. Now of course, many businesses do have high seasons, and during these times, they can add to their marketing budgets. Bumping your minimum threshold up in your busy season makes sense—pour it on for a time. It is fine to add to your marketing budget one quarter of the year, but for the other nine months, there should be no wavering from the budgeted minimum spend.

And now let's dig further into the practice of spending the minimum on marketing.

If you do spend the minimum, guess what? You may find yourself constantly stressed, asking, "How come I'm not doing as well as the business over in X-town?" The truth is, if he is spending twice what you are spending on marketing, he is essentially buying your customers. As a business owner, it never ceases: Somebody is buying your customers, or is about to.

My own father, a current multi-unit Franchisee of Retro Fitness, had to be convinced of this—this is how tough it can be to emphasize the importance of spending whatever you can *above your minimum* on marketing. My father has been a good business owner his whole life, but even so, when he went to open his first Retro Fitness gym with my brother, he thought it was fine to stick to the absolute minimum amount on marketing. He didn't understand the power of compounding in marketing. Now, my brother had spent a lot of time with me at my gyms and had watched me in action, so he knew we should have a family/business partners' sit down.

This was family, and Retro Fitness was my baby, so I said to my father and brother, "I'm not going to tell you what to do. I'm going to give you examples of what's been done." I explained that if you want to have X number of people purchase your product or service, this is how it works: You can buy them today with your marketing dollars, spending a little more money upfront, or you can buy them slowly over time. If you decide today that you want to buy customers slowly over time, two things can happen. First, let's assume you have a great product and a great brand, and you just need to expose the world to it. Once people are exposed to it, you will keep them. But if they never get exposed to your amazing product or service because they don't know you exist, all that critical time, money, and energy you have spent on your dream will be wasted. Nobody will be drinking your Kool-Aid today.

If your competitor has jumped ahead of you, all those customers will never know how great your Kool-Aid tastes, because they'll be happily sipping your competitor's. It will take those thirsty customers that much longer to first get a whiff of what flavor you are offering and then to try it and switch. So by waiting to win customers over time, you lose market-share opportunity. You can file this sub-budget expense under "Marketing: Opportunity Cost."

The second issue with choosing to market in the old-school small-budget-minded manner is that when you are starting out as a new business owner, you often don't realize the business concept of customer compounding. Let's say you are a niche health-food store. How much more could you stand to profit if even just one person were exposed to you today, rather than six months from now? The exponential factor as it relates to your ROI is incalculable. If that one person whose attention you won by beefing up your marketing budget straight out of the gate brings in just one other friend this week (referrals are the best type of new customer, by the way), word will spread—and it will spread this week instead of months down the road.

Ultimately, if you don't spend money now on reaching and buying customers, you lose out on all the money they—and their friends—could have been spending with you. Let's not forget the potential additional revenue from cross-selling this new customer into other products and services you may offer. If you ever hear me speak about marketing, you will inevitably hear me say this: "You can buy your customers today and win, or

> **Ultimately, if you don't spend money now on reaching and buying customers, you lose out on all the money they— and their friends— could have been spending with you.**

you can buy them tomorrow and wait." The trouble is, you may not be afforded the time if you decide to wait: You could go out of business!

That was the fifteen-minute conversation I had with my father and brother, and they never looked back. They went pedal to the metal with their marketing budget, and now, seven years out, their club continues to grow. They have seen competitors come and go in their market, and their clientele have stayed put because they have no incentive to go elsewhere—my father and brother run a great gym and stay relevant 365 days a year.

Go hard from the get-go, or go home. There really is no other way.

In addition to keeping your business in the eyes, hearts, and minds of your customers, smart marketing allows you to do the things you are going to need to do to stay viable down the road. Whether you need to add new products or improve your facility with a new paint job or new furniture later on, you have to spend money in marketing now to get that customer revenue now. Get customers now, make them raving fans and disciples of your business, and start making money now. Go hard from the get-go, or go home. There really is no other way.

Marketing is evolving at the speed of light. It takes more than making a first impression to stay relevant today. Every time you turn around, there is a hot new buzzword in marketing, but one constant that will never change is the importance of understanding the message you want people to receive with your marketing campaign.

...it has become easier than ever to nail down who you want to market to and who you do not want to waste a dime on. If your product is completely irrelevant to one segment of the population, you don't market to them— it is that simple.

Before you go to market, you have to know who you want to market to—for example, male Baby Boomers, female millennials, or Generation X. Once you know your budget, decide who your target customer is. Who do you want to buy your product or service? Whom do you expect to reach in the market? The better you are at identifying your ideal target customer, the better your results will be. You don't throw a ball without aiming it at its target beforehand, unless you are two years old. Nail your ideal target customer and you will win in business, day in and day out.

Research today can be done at the touch of a button, via marketing polls and studies of all kinds. Demographic analysis tools reach far beyond your customer's current city and income level. Today's business owner has access to so much information about potential customers, it has become easier than ever to nail down who you want to market to and who you do not want to waste a dime on. If your product is completely irrelevant to one segment of the population, you don't market to them—it is that simple. If your target market is senior citizens in rural areas, then you will have a completely different marketing plan than if your target market is urban-dwelling mothers of toddlers. This is basic marketing strategy, and if you are not yet on top of this, you'd better not pull out your checkbook, and certainly do not open your doors. I repeat: If you don't have a grasp on your target market, stop what you are doing and figure it out *pronto*!

Once you do figure out *whom* you want to target, you have to figure out *how* to make them pay attention. Where are your potential customers most likely to notice your advertisements? What do they read, what do they do, and what do they like? Where are their eyeballs? Where do they go? Where do they spend their time? You have to be creative and figure out how you can create a marketing piece that resonates with them. Remember, in marketing, it's not always just one big plate on the dinner table—it's many. Marketing is multiple select dishes—you want to put out the right message in the right place at the right time. Where is that urban-dwelling mother of a toddler most likely to encounter your message and take it in? Spend as much time as you need working this out thoroughly.

There are multiple environments in which to reach your target base—marketers call it *deeper impact*. Deeper impact means a customer has sampled my product or service, or has seen my billboard, my direct mail piece, and my online message. Deeper impact is the creation of a multifaceted attack. With a stellar marketing plan you know exactly what you want to do, you plan it really well, and then you roll it out. You roll out the colors and the pictures and the verbiage you have created, and you roll everything out in a precise sequence. Just watch how Apple markets—this is the level of detailed creative brilliance we can all aspire to.

People don't buy your products—*they buy the feeling they associate with the use of your products.* Your marketing has to inspire emotion, and as the one in charge of your business, you need to dictate what emotion you want to elicit. Think back to all the best Coca-Cola slogans, and those of GE, Nike, Pepperidge Farm. Why not work toward that for your own business, no matter what size you are? Wear your passion on your sleeve, and build it into your brand. Keep your marketing in front of people so that anytime they think of your product or service, they choose you. This is the "top of mind" theory, and it has tremendous value.

> **People don't buy your products—they buy the feeling they associate with the use of your products.**

Marketing is not all about drawing as many eyeballs as you can for your dollar. It's drawing the *right* eyeballs, the ones that belong to the ideal customer. Online marketing provides an inexpensive channel to the masses, but of course, with every Tom, Dick, and Harry offering to improve your SEO, you have to stay smart—do your own research first so that you don't spend half your marketing budget on so-called experts. Be smart: interview several of the thousands of online marketing companies that will help you gather data. Get references from their current clients.

Again, enough books have been written on marketing and data and customer targeting to fill an entire warehouse, but don't fret—you do not have to read every book out there. Be intelligent. Do the research until you understand how marketing works. Once you understand how to buy marketing, you can begin to talk to people and negotiate. Above all, know that your marketing campaign is representing *your brand*. Take charge.

In the beginning, you will be your own in-house marketing expert—in fact, you had better be, because who knows your brand better than you? Allow no marketer to tell you what's best for your brand. When it comes to your brand, it is the marketer's job first to listen, and then to explain to you how your vision can be turned into a money-making campaign. Your business should have a personality, and your marketing must be able to convey that personality.

When I brought in my first big marketing firm, I invited them to my vacation home, where we hung out on the deck overlooking the Atlantic Ocean. I spent hours telling them stories about the culture of Retro Fitness, who my members are, how great they are, how we interact with them inside the gym, and how I wanted my marketing to reflect that. I provide a high-value fitness center for a low cost because I want more people to join the family of Retro Fitness. Out of this discussion, my marketing team created the slogan we continue to use today: *Retro Fitness: We Get You.* And of course, it is the truth—we get our members and our members know it.

You are your business right now. You are the culture. You know your product and service and the brand you want to create. No one else can be your mouthpiece. You have to trust yourself in your process. Marketing professionals will help you with messaging, but the message needs to come from your heart.

Marketing professionals will help you with messaging, but the message needs to come from your heart.

Once you've got the slogan that reflects exactly what your business is about, *give before you ask to receive.* That is, build relationships in order to build up your marketing. If you are starting a tutoring business, for example, offer an underperforming school a few training tools for free. Once they see that your product works, they will come knocking at your door and will refer you. Make it worth their while. Once you see some success, take your giving one step further—sponsor a few community activities through the school, or sponsor a local sports team.

By giving before you receive, you not only gain eyeballs on your business, but you also generate goodwill that will ripple forward into the future. Goodwill keeps you relevant, because people like it when you support their community, and they will support you in turn. Always earmark part of your marketing budget for activities and outreach that show your commitment to the place where you are doing business.

All marketing is relevant—from the high-tech advertising blitz to the logo on the dugout of your local Little League team. Marketing is short-term, mid-term, and long-term—that is, all of it has a shelf life. Today you might offer an electronic coupon with a QR code your customers can scan. Tomorrow, you might send out a flyer in the mail. Your billboard may stay up the entire year. Different types of marketing will generate different impacts on different types of consumers—and the point is, you need all of it; you need the balance.

Do spend at least ten percent of your budget on marketing twelve months a year, but aim to do slightly more. Do not fret too much about the distant future, and never underestimate the power of one customer won today. Show customers the heart and soul of your company, and turn their commitment

to you into a thousand positive Tweets or Yelp reviews. Today, the satisfied customer is one of your mightiest marketing tools. Generate goodwill and watch your marketing dollar expand exponentially. Do not cut a single corner.

TAKEAWAY

- Marketing is your most important expense. It must be the first thing added to your budget when you are starting out, and the last thing cut when times are hard.

  *What are **you** willing to spend on marketing?*

CHAPTER SEVEN

True Entrepreneurs Can't Stop!

WHEN MOST people talk about entrepreneurs, they talk about the big ones like Jeff Bezos and Elon Musk. Bezos and Musk are our modern day heroes, our great visionaries. They have not only smarts, but also the entrepreneurial spirit. They create things we hardly even knew we needed or wanted. Of course, there are a thousand other entrepreneurs out there doing brilliant things, and although we don't talk about them as much, they are driving amazing new businesses and products.

The entrepreneur must not only be creative, but driven. Again, you could come up with the best tasting Kool-Aid since the original formula, but if you don't put your product in front of people before somebody else does, nobody will know how delicious it is. You have to be driven. You have to say, "Okay, I thought of this wonderful thing, and I am going to take it out into the world because I know that everyone will love it

> ...I tell people I meet and train, "If you have an idea that everyone is calling 'crazy,' chances are, it is going to turn out to be extraordinary."

as much as I do." It is not enough in entrepreneurship to be a creative genius. You have to understand how to take something great and do something great with it. When Steve Jobs thought of the iPod, he created not just another MP3 player, but a category and a brand the whole world would forever want a piece of. That's what Elon Musk did too: He thought, *I wish I had a car that wasn't reliant on fuel, and I think everyone else does, too.* Now Musk is building rocket ships that do things no rocket ships have ever done before.

Thinking the way Musk and Jobs thought, and then acting upon those thoughts, takes a certain personality. When I first started Retro Fitness, I started with the belief that affordable fitness was important. I assumed everyone else wanted the same thing. "You might not make it," a friend of mine said, "It sounds crazy."

Now I tell people I meet and train, "If you have an idea that everyone is calling 'crazy,' chances are, it is going to turn out to be extraordinary."

Retro Fitness turned out to be extraordinary. *Crazy*, in my book, is the barometer of *potential greatness*. If people are telling you your idea sounds "kind of cool," that means the product is going to be good. Now, good isn't bad—you could make millions of dollars just being good. But extraordinary is what you want, right? That's what everybody wants.

Look, everybody thought Jobs was kooky—in fact, at one point in his career, he was fired from his own company. Politicians think Elon Musk is crazy—they fear him. So, if your friends and competitors and politicians and colleagues are telling you you're nuts, chances are you are really on to something.

It is important to understand the naysayers. They inevitably show up when you are about to start anything new. At times, all you will have to battle them with is your passion. If you shut your brilliant idea down after the first person says, "You must be off your rocker!" your brilliant idea will never see the light of day. If you scare easily, you have a problem. Naysayers will be many, and they will come in many guises, but if you believe with all your heart in your product or service, you will have the drive to get you through your first "No way!" and past the many naysayers who are going to be smacking you in the face along the way.

Once you decide you are going to build that

> ...once you get the ball rolling, the obstacles will only get bigger, and if you are not strong-willed and passionate, you are setting yourself up for trouble.

electric car, you have to imagine how many obstacles will present themselves, and you have to check in with yourself: Do you have the personality and drive to conquer those challenges? Are you willing to change an entire industry, as Jobs did and as Musk and Bezos are doing? Because once you get the ball rolling, the obstacles will only get bigger, and if you are not strong-willed and passionate, you are setting yourself up for trouble.

Drive and passion separate the great entrepreneurs from the rest of the folks doing business. The great entrepreneurs believe in what they do. "You want to smack me along the way?" says the great entrepreneur. "Go ahead. But what you don't realize is the wind generated by all your smacking will become the wind in my sails." Entrepreneurs can't stop. They may be considered cocky or kooky or difficult, but all are good signs in my book.

There is no such thing as downtime for the entrepreneur. Not only do they not stop at the first *no*, they do not stop at the first business idea or concept or product. They don't say or listen to "no," all the way down the line. They get bitten by the fever of, "Yes, this is amazing and possible!" and the fever never goes away. I have jokingly told my accountant that I wanted to write off toilet paper as a business expense, because I talk about my business even when I am in the bathroom. Wherever I go, I am talking about my businesses. It's what entrepreneurs do—we are always telling and selling our business.

It does help that I am a natural born talker, of course, but I remember reading somewhere that no matter where you are, you should always tell ten people what you do. Now, if you are a doctor at a cocktail party, of course, this idea can work against you. Everybody wants to ask you about an ailment they have, and you wind up spending the entire party diagnosing. But if you are in business, whether you are waiting in a doctor's office or in a grocery store line, start talking.

When I first started with Retro Fitness, I'd be out and about chatting with people and I would simply say, "Hey, you look like you work out. Where do you work out?" If they were already members of Retro Fitness, we had a wonderful conversation. If they were members at a competitor's place, I would tell them who I was and then hand them my card, which always has a free pass. "Come on in and try us," I would say.

Early on, you learn to always carry your business card with you, and that card should contain your website and contact information, plus a coupon for your product. Always be prepared to share your passion, your stories, and your product.

It all goes back to in-person marketing and balance. Writing off your toilet paper might be a reach (no pun intended), but indeed, you make connections wherever and whenever you can—without becoming ceaselessly annoying. You can turn off your business talk at times, but when you love something as much as you love your business, it isn't easy. You go out to an anniversary dinner with your spouse, and you can't help but study the cleanliness of the place or the attire of the staff. Information from all businesses feeds your brain—that always-observing and learning part of your brain—but when your spouse reaches over to hold your hand, it is okay to shift gears.

You are constantly talking and thinking about your business, not because you are self-absorbed or obsessed, but because you want to share it with people, especially the ones you care about. You want the world to enjoy your business as much as you do. When I was just starting out with Retro Fitness, I took my kids with me because I wanted them to see the people and the culture there, to understand it. Who wouldn't want to put fitness in the minds of their children? Who wouldn't want members of their business community to know a little bit about the person they are beyond the entrepreneur?

You share what you love with your family, and you share what you love with society at large.

I wanted to share my business with my family because someday, who knows, maybe one of my children will own or run their own Retro Fitness. You share what you love with your family, and you share what you love with society at large. Some entrepreneurs share technology; others share health. My oldest daughter wants to be an animator for Disney, and I tell her, "Go for it! Disney's a great innovative company if there ever was one." But in the meantime, growing up, maybe my daughter will use her creative skills to design some logos for one of my companies.

Understand that at some point you alone no longer represent your brand—after you get started, your employees and your customers represent it too. If you are giving away free t-shirts with your logo on them, which we do when somebody joins the gym, you'd better give them a quality t-shirt. If you give out anything that falls apart and looks shabby after the first wash, remember that you might have customers out there wearing your logo ... and ruining your curb appeal from afar.

Never being able to stop being an entrepreneur once you become one is similar to never being able to stop being a parent once you become one: You have to be extremely protective, and very careful about where and how your company is represented. You have to keep an eye out for any misuse or abuse of your logo and your brand, and when necessary, take legal action.

> **You have to keep an eye out for any misuse or abuse of your logo and your brand, and when necessary, take legal action. Your reputation and future are at stake because *your brand is you.***

Your reputation and future are at stake because *your brand is you.* Remember what we said in an earlier chapter: Curb appeal starts outside your front door; it starts with you if you are wearing your brand or talking about it. Look the part. Have yourself together. The public will associate how you take care of yourself with how you run your business. Step up your game.

Sometimes your business motivates you to become a better person, because all of a sudden, there is a lot more at stake. Have you ever noticed that people behave more nicely when they are at Disneyworld? It's an interesting phenomenon, and it happens because there is a culture going on at Disney. Disney is a business that changes you as a person, even if just temporarily. Your business can do that too. Tuck your shirt in, put a belt on, make sure your shoes are shined and your clothes are clean, and share your passion and knowledge with a smile.

If you want to run your own show, it's time to put your big boy or big girl pants on. The two events in my life that urged me to own up to adulthood were the opening of my first business and the birth of my first child. I'm thankful every day that I first learned the lessons of adulthood in business—the responsibility is enormous. It is also exciting and liberating.

The point is, do not be afraid to toy with new ideas and new responsibilities. Don't be afraid to be called obsessive or crazy. Never stop paying attention to the details—and not only your own. There is no downtime for the entrepreneur. You are constantly asking questions and answering them. You are always sharing with others and always asking experts to share with you. Not a natural born talker? Learn where and when and how to talk in spurts, if you must … because you must. I was a great talker, but I learned to be a great communicator through training.

People will be dealing with your product, sometimes at a granular level. When you first start out you will be overwhelmed with excitement, but don't race forward too fast when it comes to details. It might take you two weeks to decide on the color of your countertops for just one small section of a lavatory after looking at thousands of samples. Is the color appealing? Does water spot and stain on this surface? Does it wipe down easily? What does it look like over time? Pay attention, because if you plan on being around for a while, the time and money you spend on the minutiae now will be well spent. You will spend money again to fix or change out those countertops one day, I promise. It might not be tomorrow or next week, but five years from now, rushing will cost you.

Paying attention to details before you start is critical. Know that you will have to fix some of those details along the way, because when you start, you never get it 100 percent right. You aim for 100 percent, and will hopefully reach 95, fixing that other 5 percent eventually. It may seem silly to lose sleep over a $200 detail after spending $1 million to build your business, but you will. In my case, silly as it sounds, it was our gyms' garbage cans. I had to change them all to red, simply because the color looked nicer and blended into our color scheme. This is the psychotic level of detail entrepreneurs talk about—the kind of detail we cannot stop talking about. Did I mention I had those red garbage cans delivered overnight the day after we opened?

In the grand scheme of things, at a gym for example, where garbage cans are necessary to dispose of used paper towels and so on, granular details always matter. As the owner of any business, you can't stop obsessing over what you can do to make the customer experience better. And your customers will love you for paying that level of attention. They may never notice that you switched out the cheaper green garbage cans for more expensive and attractive red ones, but keep in mind that you aren't necessarily making changes in order to get compliments; you are making changes to avoid complaints—even if sometimes, the complaints are your own.

When you really love and respect your business, it shows. In Tom Connellan's book, *Inside the Magic Kingdom: Seven Keys to Disney's Success*, he describes the close attention Disney pays to the hitching posts that line its streets. On a regular basis, the posts are changed and painted, depending on wear. This obsession with detail, as you can imagine, is something I absolutely admire about the Disney brand. In fact, after reading this book, I was inspired to implement a timeline for when Retro Fitness gyms are to repaint the common areas of the facilities. Again, because a gym is a high-touch environment, sometimes it isn't about what garners compliments, but about what does not garner complaints—or lost customers. When you love what you do and where you go to work every day, you take pride in every detail. You will hear about something Disney or Apple does, and you will put that genius to work for your own business. You will create an environment in which people want to spend their time and money. And always, you will be thinking of the next great idea.

TAKEAWAYS

- Your business and your brand are part of your identity as a person; be protective of them, even down to small details.
- Always carry business cards.

CHAPTER EIGHT

If Obstacles Don't Make You Furious, Then You Just Don't Care Enough

ONE PERSON'S biggest challenge doesn't even make it onto another person's radar, which makes challenges an interesting and never-ending topic. There are challenges—minor and major—at every stage of entrepreneurship, but of course, that is part of the lure for the entrepreneur.

As an entrepreneur, you have to think like a top athlete: If you come to the game thinking, "I can't win this," then you have already lost. Ultimately, your state of mind is more important than the challenges themselves. The mindset you need before the doors even open to your business is this: *Challenges exist. They will come. Things will sometimes be out of my control, so, I will focus on controlling what I can. When I run into an obstacle, I will first identify it, and then decide how best to manage it.*

> **In order to tackle challenges from a place of confidence, we must be prepared. Of course, you can't prepare for every single thing that could possibly go wrong, but you can absolutely prepare for how you will handle problems.**

In business, you are dealing with human beings—offer them a smile. Say "please" and "thank you." You can't control the weather on opening day, but you can control how you and your employees greet customers. You can influence people. You can overcome challenges by meeting them with as level a head as possible. No, you can't always "keep calm and carry on," because of course, you are passionate—you need your passion more than ever when challenges arise. But it is best to remember that we all make much better decisions and think much more efficiently after taking a deep breath or two—and repeating to ourselves, "Keep calm and carry on" one or two times before acting.

In order to tackle challenges from a place of confidence, we must be prepared. Of course, you can't prepare for every single thing that could possibly go wrong, but you can absolutely prepare for how you will handle problems. When something difficult is thrown in your lap, you have to plan to take it in stride. If you flip out and run around screaming, "Holy cow, the sky is falling!" every time a crisis occurs, you will burn out. You and your business will fail.

Obstacles come in all shapes and sizes, but first and foremost, you need to plan how you will attack them. You have to think aggressively, but act calmly, that is, you cannot let anything impede your forward momentum or dampen your optimism—not when you first open your doors, and not years down the road, when the obstacles will be different. Running your business is like running a marathon, and if you don't handle obstacles as they come, you will begin to feel like you are running with fifteen-pound weights strapped to your ankles. Having no plan for how to handle obstacles will slow you down, and eventually break you.

> Running your business is like running a marathon, and if you don't handle obstacles as they come, you will begin to feel like you are running with fifteen-pound weights strapped to your ankles.

Consciously cultivate a levelheaded mindset early on, in order to build your mental endurance. From time to time, yes, you may flip out in private. You may sit back in your office chair and wonder, "Why am I doing this?" Obstacles and challenges will try to work their way into your psyche and may extinguish some of your fire. Only with the right mindset will you be able to keep it burning. You must relight the flames—your business is your heart and soul.

Maintaining a big-picture perspective helps. When you hit an obstacle—say it rains torrentially during your grand opening—you need to ask yourself: Is this the end of the world? Will I possibly use this anecdote to help some other enthusiastic entrepreneur build the life of his dreams one day? If we get through this, can we continue? The answer to all of the above is usually, "Of course!"

In five years, the challenges you faced on opening day or in that first year will be old news. You will be an expert at handling those minor issues. When you are an entrepreneur, you have *your mind set and your mindset*—come what may. Everybody is relying on you. If you come to the game with your head in the sand, where do you think your employees' heads are going to go—or worse, your customers? When you are the business owner, your posture is being watched by everyone around you. You are the leader. Your persona will either be really good for your business or really bad. This success or failure, awareness or denial, is something you can control. Be intelligent about how you handle obstacles, and how you train the people around you to handle them.

"If XYZ happens, what will I do and what will my employees do?" Write down three or four actions to take. The first one might be as simple as, "Step away from the challenge for a moment." Getting a bit of distance, even if just for a few minutes, can allow you to make room for something positive to focus on, and can diffuse some of the emotion that arises in any challenging situation. This will allow you to better dictate your state. Even the best and most seasoned entrepreneurs, when we are too emotional or negative in our thinking, risk making bad choices. Whatever it takes to get out of that unstable frame of mind, do it, and then say, "OK, this is happening. I can deal with this. I have to get ABC done. What resources do I need?"

> Getting a bit of distance, even if just for a few minutes, can allow you to make room for something positive to focus on, and can diffuse some of the emotion that arises in any challenging situation.

We spent an entire chapter on the importance of being resourceful—and certainly when obstacles appear, you have to be resourceful. During a challenge, this is what resourceful looks like: "What do I have to do, and who do I need? What is the outcome I need to aim for right now?" You then go to your game plan. You remind yourself of the big picture—five years from now, this will be water under the bridge, so long as you deal effectively and efficiently with the burst dam now.

If the challenge requires you, and only you, to do something, do it. If the challenge is out of your personal realm of expertise, start making some calls. Call your marketing company, your vendors, your IT expert, or whomever you have deemed appropriate for the task at hand, and get them to do what they do best. Just take action.

Every challenge has a conclusion. As an entrepreneur, you will constantly ask yourself, "What is the necessary outcome? What do I need to have settled on the other side of this challenge?" You may need to fix or buy a new work van, or you may need to fire someone—the important thing is to realize that every challenge is more than just a task. Every challenge has an end point, and it is up to you to identify that endpoint and solve the problem.

You will note that when it comes to problem solving, I usually recommend asking yourself questions first. The capacity of our brains is amazing, so remember, whatever you ask your brain, it will give you a response. Ask a bad question—expect a terrible answer; ask a good question—you catch my drift. Ask excellent questions when trying to solve challenges.

You are up for any challenge; I know this, because you have gotten this far in this book. Perseverance is a requirement in our world. Once you have a system in place for solving problems and overcoming obstacles, you have won half of any battle. Combine that with your perseverance, and you have a substantial upper hand.

If you do your research, and if you reach out and talk to experts and you utilize your resources—if you incorporate everything in this book into your mindset and game plan—you will be able to maintain your enthusiasm in good times and bad. Your confidence will grow with each obstacle you crush. Whether the obstacles come at you all at once or one after the other, you will address them, and you will address them quickly. One of my favorite authors, Zig Ziglar, once said, "If you're going to have to swallow a frog, you don't want to have to look at that sucker too long."

Sometimes too, the most dangerous obstacles are the ones that at first do not seem like challenges—these are the situations in which you think, "No problem, I'll get to this later. I'll do this tomorrow." Pay attention to those types of

> **What success comes down to, ultimately, is overcoming yourself. This is your biggest challenge, and you will be tested again and again.**

obstacles, because they can sneak up on you and come back much bigger than they first appeared. Challenges—even those that don't appear urgent—can turn into ankle weights, slowly sucking your time and energy and passion. Travel light.

There are so many challenges in business—I could write a book on each and every one. There are so many variables. You may be on your first business or your fifth. Getting started is a challenge; staying alive is a challenge; going from good to great is a challenge. Step into the game, conquer your fears, gain experience and confidence—and accept that none of this comes naturally or all at once. Yes, we are gifted, many of us, with this entrepreneurial spirit, but we are human too. We need, like everyone else, to feel good about what we are doing. When the obstacles come, if we don't have it in us to fight tooth and nail for our livelihood, for our dreams, for our heart and soul—for our business—we are in big trouble.

What success comes down to, ultimately, is overcoming yourself. This is your biggest challenge, and you will be tested again and again. When in doubt, reread your business plan. If you love that plan and can stand behind it, chances are that somebody else will too—some bank will, an investor will, loyal customers will. Take comfort in knowing you are not the first person to try what you are trying. You are in great company—there are thousands of successful entrepreneurs who are exceeding their original dreams today because they got past their early doubts and overcame challenges.

It is unlikely that you will just start your business and go—there is rarely smooth sailing right out of the gate. You have to be willing to sacrifice a little bit at every stage of the game, reaching out of your comfort zone. When you have missed the third family barbeque because you are enthusiastically pursuing your entrepreneurial dream, you are on the right track. Balance will come, but not at first. A first challenge to getting your business going will be the temporary sacrifices you will make, and this can be overwhelming. You will have your family and friends—and your dreams for your business—but early on, something will have to give.

When your business is up and running, when you are comfortable and things are going well, when some of the balance does get restored, *bam*—the challenge then becomes, "How do I get better?" You are good, but how do you become great? Good enough is enough for some people, but really, you want to be great. How do you get there? What do you have to do? How do you resist resting in the comfort zone? Do you expand to another location, develop your online business, or revamp your product line? Do you have the right people working with you? Did your wife just have a baby?

> **At some point in business, you will have to let other people do some of the things that you were doing in order to grow and flourish. ... It is inevitable.**

It's at the three- to five-year mark, usually, that real life begins to rear its head again. You've made it work, your business is growing—so you have some new decisions to make. Can you start delegating to someone else? Do you trust someone else? At some point in business, you will have to let other people do some of the things that you were doing in order to grow and flourish. There are only so many hours in the day, and now you will be challenged by the time and trust quandary. It is inevitable.

Again, the sheer number of challenges facing the entrepreneur could fill an entire encyclopedia set. Some challenges are typical of all businesses, new or existing, big or small, retail or non-retail, and so on. The point is, you have to realize how important obstacles are. When you are excited about your business and an obstacle threatens your end result, you must be prepared to throw it out of the way, not push it out of the way. You will want to have a plan that entails taking a few moments to get your mind right when faced with an obstacle, but you had also better be prepared to treat obstacles as if they were thieves or murderers set on trampling your dreams.

TAKEAWAYS

- When obstacles appear, they must be taken seriously and dealt with swiftly.
- If you do not have the expertise necessary to handle an obstacle, call someone who does.

What kinds of obstacles have you faced in your professional life? How did you overcome them?

CHAPTER NINE

There's (Almost) No Such Thing as Growing Too Quickly

THE NEED to be level-headed and fast when dealing with obstacles is one thing. Speed, in terms of creating and managing growth, is an entirely different beast. Common wisdom may say, "Moderate your growth," or "Don't expand to quickly." I say, "Do not listen to anyone who tells you that."

You already know that half of what you learn in the business school textbooks and lectures will fly right out the door when you begin doing real-life business. It is the contacts you make everywhere you go, talking about your business and asking other entrepreneurs about theirs, that will help you most along your way. All these analysts talk about rate of growth, and while I appreciate their input, it does not jibe with my experience of what works best. If you want to try "slow-paced growth" because that is what the talking heads on TV are promoting, or because that lingo is trending on Twitter, let

> **What will happen if you follow the slow or moderate growth plan is this: Your competitor is going to come in and eat your lunch before you can.**

me tell you to think again—think outside that box. This is what entrepreneurs must do. Analysts look at the past and make decisions; entrepreneurs look into the future and do the same.

What will happen if you follow the slow or moderate growth plan is this: Your competitor is going to come in and eat your lunch before you can. Someone else is always fighting for your customers' eyeballs. If you say, "Well, I want to move into the town next door—I have the money and the capacity—but I'm going to wait," my advice is to adapt your timeline. Do not wait. If you have a great product, protect your investment by closing the gates of the market. Own the market.

Slow growth can be dangerous. If your product is good, someone will copy it, and they will move their business right into your neighborhood, or to the neighborhood you are waiting to expand into. I see this happen every single day, in every kind of business, including my own. The people who understand and live by spreadsheets do not necessarily understand the tide of emotion behind business. Predictable calculations are one thing, but more often than not, they mean nothing in the real world. They cannot account for the incalculable and the intangibles in business. Emotion is what controls and changes everything in business.

Your product will do really well, or really poorly, regardless of numbers in a column. Synergy is everything in business. Your product may take on its own personality. People may become really excited by your product overnight—based on one celebrity linking to it, or one Tweet going viral. Emotion and excitement create business now more than ever, and so all these people whose job it is analyze business and business growth … well, let them keep doing their jobs. The truth is, business is unpredictable.

> **Synergy is everything in business. … The truth is, business is unpredictable.**

Say you are a great dry cleaner. You work with the best products, and people are going wild over some new process you use that prolongs the life of their clothes and is environmentally friendly. They will drive half an hour to use your services—but they wish you would open a location closer to them. You have the resources, but you are stuck in the old "slow growth" belief system. Well, I have a newsflash for you: Someone will open a location closer to some of your customers if you don't. Someone will take some of your current customer base, even if they are not as good as you, because location equals convenience.

Don't delude yourself, thinking, *My product is better. People will continue to drive farther.* They won't. Even when it comes to birthday cakes for their children, the majority of people will drive ten minutes for a decent cake before they will drive thirty for a great cake. So, if you have that great product, spread it as far and as wide as you can—ride your first wave of greatness, reinvest, use all the tools and tactics I have given you, and expand as quickly as possible.

Timing in relation to growth and expansion all comes down to how resourceful you are. Do you have enough assets that the bank will lend you more money? Do you have people who want to invest because they see lines out your door? Don't get caught saying, "I have the money, but I don't have the expertise." If you don't have the expertise, reach out to those who do. Leap further! Today's technology allows for quick but efficient growth—take advantage of them.

Once your first business is doing really well—once you are the dry cleaning master or the birthday cake king—go back to your plan. If you have the willingness and a plan, someone is going to walk in your door and say, "I would love to open up one of these stores. How do I get involved? When and where are you expanding?" That should be your expectation when you have that product people love—the one they have become fanatical about overnight. "Where else can I find you and how soon?"

How many of you wished you could open a Chipotle or Starbucks in your town or city, only to find out they are all company-owned and not franchisable? When a business is awesome, everyone wants a piece of it.

When you get into business, you should be thinking big, no matter what. You start with one business, but as soon as it is churning, you are looking at locations two, ten, and fifteen miles away. What was your dream? You started your own business, created systems within that business, sacrificed, delegated, and piled on the successes. If you're able to do all that, why not do more? Why wait two years to go to town X if your business is blowing competitors out of the water today? Why let one of your competitors take town X?

If your product is great, and you are diversifying your bucket by having multiple stores, then you are also protecting your investment. If stores in towns X and Y end up doing really well, and the one in town

Having multiple locations is helpful because you have other baskets to pull from.

Z ends up struggling, X and Y will carry Z. Having multiple locations is helpful because you have other baskets to pull from. Yes, growing your business requires a larger investment, but it also creates a bigger catch and a bigger safety net. This could pay large dividends when you finally decide to exit. With diligent, educated planning, growth does not have to

> **Rapid growth is not the same as haphazard growth—I am against the chicken-with-its-head-cut-off approach to anything.**

take time.

Today's technology can enable you to quickly and easily evaluate another location from the comfort of your own office. How many households, schools, and incomes over $100,000 are there? What is the average age and gender of residents? You can get layers and layers of demographic information. You can use free and paid services to find locations, and to negotiate. Rapid growth is not the same as haphazard growth—I am against the chicken-with-its-head-cut-off approach to anything. Have a plan and use your resources. Technology is swift, and customers are swift—stay in the game and improve upon it. Use speed and diligence in everything you do.

If you start slowing down your decision-making processes, check in on your mindset. Have you become your own obstacle? Don't you be the chokehold that stifles your own business growth. Fast growth depends on how you handle yourself. Strive for efficiency—remember that just as when we discussed working with obstacles, working with speed does not mean working in a manical state of mind. You have to be smart about how you manage your cash flow when you start making money. I've said it before, but it bears repeating: You should be putting money aside for your next stage of growth—this will allow you to move with the necessary swiftness. This will allow you to move into that up-and-coming neighborhood before your competitor gets there. With your cash resources saved, you are in a position to make more decisions. What better position is there to be in? Be very aware that success in business lulls many people to sleep. You get comfortable, and then you get lazy. You can't let this happen.

The naysayers of business are the people who dislike you for who you are today—they don't want you to change. "Slow and easy," they say. They don't want you go to away; they want you to stay. They like you the way you are, and are afraid of losing *the you of today*. This is normal behavior from friends and family, so be patient with them. What I would say to them is, "Here is where I am headed, here is who I am going to be. I'd appreciate your ongoing support. Join me in bringing this dream to life."

Some of the naysayers have tried and failed, and some have never tried at all. They are not you though, and they are not reading books like the one in your hands. They are not learning what you are learning and doing what you are doing. The fact that you are holding this book says something about you right now: it says that you care about doing the research before starting your own business, and you want to make money. You want to be in charge of your own journey and freedom. As you've seen so far, this requires walking a fine line between gusto and passion, between patience and planning. You'll walk that line, you'll toe that line, and you'll redraw it after each and every success and learning experience you tally.

TAKEAWAYS

- There is no such thing as growing too fast. Never let anyone tell you different.
- If you hesitate when the opportunity to expand presents itself, a competitor will eat your lunch.

CHAPTER TEN

The Work/Life Balance Isn't Always Easy for People Like Us

THE BIGGEST pitfall for a lot of entrepreneurs is believing they are achieving a work-life balance when in fact, they are not managing the life factor attentively enough. When you are passionate about your business, you can reach a state of fulfillment by attending solely to your business's needs. It's exciting, starting your own business—and it gets more exciting when things start going well.

When you first set out to build or rebuild the life you want, family, friends, and hobbies fall by the wayside more often than not. The "life" sacrifices are a necessity at times—but they should be temporary. The trick is to figure out when the work/life imbalance is tipping dangerously, in order to prevent it from irreversibly or permanently ruining everything around you. You will fall in love with your business; your business will become your mistress. The trick is to build that future so that everyone you love and cherish will benefit from it, while keeping everyone in line with your vision at times when they feel forgotten or neglected. The key is to remind everyone—including yourself—that you are ultimately striving for the kind of freedom you can share with everyone you care about—the kind of freedom only a business owner can have.

Your business should fulfill you. You want your business to have a personality you love, care for, and thrive on. You should feel entirely consumed by it. What you want to avoid is becoming deluded by it. When your business begins to erode your time and your freedom—the very things you were aiming for when you started it—you need to take a few deep breaths and step back from the situation. Think. Realize that your business is a vehicle for success.

Your business is meant to offer you power, freedom, and the ability to give more. In the last chapter we talked about challenges such as doubt, fear, money, competition, and hiring people you trust, but the work/life balance is one challenge that presents itself constantly with entrepreneurship, in ways it never did when you were working for someone else.

There is an addictive element to success. You sit back after your first year and say, "Holy cow, I did this much! Just think what could happen if I put two more hours in every other day, or five more days a month."

When the business is successful, it becomes a totally different animal. "More" becomes elusive, and you get hungrier to chase it. Finding a healthy life balance isn't easy for anyone, but you can see how for the entrepreneur, it is a particularly hard struggle. You want to create endless capacity in your business, but you also have to constantly check in with yourself and ask, "Am I spending more time on this than I thought I was going to? Am I spending more

When the business is successful, it becomes a totally different animal. "More" becomes elusive, and you get hungrier to chase it.

time on this than is necessary? Am I crossing into 'too much time' territory? Can I delegate or outsource some of this, and see my family tonight?"

With each goal met, more are set. But unless you have no other obligations in the world, at a certain point you have to draw a line in the sand. For me, when I started out my business was fitness. I have always loved working out and spending time in gyms, and I loved the people there, so my hobby was inside my business. I could have lived in the locker room if I had set up a bed there. I visited the gym, built relationships at the gym, showered at the gym, and even ate there. I even had a baby swing in my office at the gym for my first daughter. Ask any entrepreneur, and he or she will sound almost as psychotic as I once was.

The doctor, the lawyer, and the city worker don't weave their lives into their careers like the entrepreneur does. When it is going really well, you want to always be there. You don't go to Disney's Magic Kingdom and leave before the fireworks. That's anticlimactic. At the same time, when times are tough or tight, you *have* to be there. You don't leave your baby stranded. And then there are the days when you come home and don't want to talk about any of it—the good or the bad. You are so over the edge you can't even answer the question, "How was your day?"

It took me a while to acknowledge I was not quite mastering the work/life balance—it took having children. When my first two children were toddlers, I was busy building my business. They were in that swing in my office, but until I finally figured out some of the lessons laid out in this book, I wasn't spending enough time with the people who mattered to me most. My wife supported me and knew that sooner rather than later I would see the light. She knew I was immersed in my work because I loved it, but it wasn't until our third and fourth children came along that I finally mastered my own obsession. I had grown my business beyond my wildest expectations because of those first few years of sacrifice and setting everything else aside—it was time to reap what I had sowed and treat my wife and children to family time that included me as a husband and father. The temporary insanity—which I occasionally dip back into—is totally worth the ability I now have to give my family anything they want in the world.

Now I coach one of my son's baseball teams and drive my daughter to school every day, but for the first two years of my business, I was failing my family. I acknowledge that now, and I write about it and talk about it in order to try to spare others from pushing the life/work imbalance too far, for too long.

> The work/life balance can be viewed as a pendulum: it will swing. The key is not to let that pendulum swing itself out of whack, into dysfunction.

Yes, there will be times you lean too hard into your work. Yes, there will be times you find yourself pleading with family and friends to understand and bear with you: "I am doing this for you," you will explain. But check in with yourself consistently and make sure you are doing what you are doing for the right reasons, and that you aren't losing sight of what is truly valuable in life. Understand that success in the business world isn't worth a hill of beans if you have no one to share it with. The work/life balance can be viewed as a pendulum: it will swing. The key is not to let that pendulum swing itself out of whack, into dysfunction.

It is easy to become egocentric when your customers love you, when have raving fans, when you are smashing the competition left and right, and when you are filling your coffers. But remember, those who are raving about your business today may not be around six months from now. When that punch in the gut comes, you will want your real life—your non-business life—to be there for you. If you have ignored it and allowed it to become anemic, you will be miserable and alone. If you have allowed your business to ruin your marriage or your friendships, you got it wrong. And for what?

Walking through a cemetery, you never read on any headstone: *John Doe. Made Ten of Millions of Dollars.* What you read is: *John Doe. Loving father. Loving husband. Best friend.* Entrepreneurship is about work and life, and work and life are about legacy. Your legacy is not a number; it is who you were as a human being. I am writing this book with the most driven and passionate audience in mind, but I stress this: What will always be remembered and admired are the relationships you built with people. How you treated all those you came into contact with in business and in your personal life will be discussed for years. In the early days of starting your business, when everyone expects you to be obsessed and slightly possessed, through the days of finding success and wanting more, the challenge will be to keep the bigger picture in mind—the long-term. The headstone.

This long view of life does not mean that your business can't be part of your legacy—financially, you hope it will. You may start a business with future generations in mind, hoping your children and grandchildren will participate and enjoy the fruits of your labor. But ultimately what most people care about—the success story they love to hear and carry on—is

that someone they loved and admired created what they created out of love and passion, and not out of ego and greed.
It's that simple. You will work infinitely harder to succeed
when you are doing it for people you care about, and not just
yourself.

In the beginning, you will be driven to achieve. And then
you will achieve, and you will begin to ask yourself *why* you
are doing what you are doing. Asking "why" brings forth some
interesting answers. In fact *why* is by far one of the most powerful questions we can ask.

When you know the reasons why you are doing something, you inevitably come up with the *what* and the *how*. I
first learned about the power of why at a very young age, at a
seminar led by Anthony Robbins, and I always come back to
it. Digging deep into that one small word leads you to your
purpose in life, and trust me, if you find your purpose in life

has no legs, you will begin to wobble. If the deepest purpose you can muster is *money*, you have constructed a table with two legs. It won't hold a thing; it will fall over.

Purpose comes out of passion: I want to create this business so that I have the financial freedom to buy my family a second home in our favorite vacation spot. We will spend our summers there. That is the work/life balance. Put your purpose down on paper, and review it at least once a day. Perhaps you'll want to review your "deep goals" yearly, but all goals should be logged and evaluated on a regular basis. I keep a Goal Book, and I open it every single day. Daily, I check and update my daily, weekly, and monthly goals. Periodically, I ask myself *why* that goal is—or is no longer—relevant.

Why was it important to me to write this book? Sharing knowledge is important to me. When I was a young entrepreneur, I had an insatiable appetite for business knowledge. I reached out to those with experience and wisdom for any nugget of usable information. Now I've got some of that to pass along to others, so they can do great things in their lives and make the country better and stronger. Writing this book now is tied to a deep goal—had I written one ten years ago, it would have been driven by ego.

Zig Ziglar had it absolutely right when he said, "You can have everything you want in life, if you will just help enough people get what they want."

Today I am winning in the work/life cycle. I have gone through a multitude of challenges, and have come out on the other end thriving. Don't get me wrong—I still struggle here and there. But today's challenges don't remotely compare to the challenges I faced when I first started. Theoretically, you could get a few of the other chapters in this book wrong and still do okay in business. If you don't get this chapter right though, you will not win. You will be nothing more than a one-hit-wonder, because you will exhaust yourself, lose your friends, spouse and kids, and probably have to pay for attorneys to sort out the mess.

As an entrepreneur, the first question you want to ask yourself when you are starting out is, "Why?" And then you never want to stop asking that question. If you have really meaningful goals, it doesn't matter if you get to them the moment you set this book down, or in five years, as long as you are setting goals. Put some big life goals on paper and start breaking them down into years, months, and weeks. What are your expectations? Who are the people in your life you care most about, and what do you want for them? What contribution do you want to make to your community, your city or region, and your country? What do you want your legacy to be?

> As an entrepreneur, the first question you want to ask yourself when you are starting out is, "Why?" And then you never want to stop asking that question.

As an entrepreneur and business owner, you can take charge of all of the above. You just have to remember to take time away from your business too, so that you can get on with all the other things that are important to you. There is not a single person who ever wished on their deathbed that they had spent more time at work.

TAKEAWAY

- Money isn't everything. The entire reason you work hard to succeed is so that you can share your success with your family.
  Have you hugged your spouse today?

CHAPTER ELEVEN

Get on Your Horse and Ride!

FROM THE start, I have been extremely fortunate. My wife has always been supportive, and my children have blown tons of wind into my sails. My wife always says, "There's nothing you can't do, you know that, right?" And my children are my biggest cheerleaders. There is no greater reward than sharing your triumphs with those you love; there would be no greater tragedy than hitting your highest business peak but losing everything around you. I hope when you reach your first peak, you can say to yourself, "I'm doing really well. What can I do equally well?"

Success breeds success and reduces stress; it acts as a kind of an outlet. People don't get much more motivated and Type A than me, and I am telling you, stress sometimes catches the best of us. There is kryptonite out there for everyone. Success means you can take some much-needed time for yourself to

> **Going the distance requires taking time to sit and *just be*, too. Supremely passionate entrepreneurs are often the square pegs in a round-hole world, and for this reason, we have to take time out to recharge.**

reenergize—to recharge the batteries, as they say. Maintaining the life/business balance so that you can get on your horse and ride long distance is not easy.

Going the distance requires taking time to sit and *just be*, too. Supremely passionate entrepreneurs are often the square pegs in a round-hole world, and for this reason, we have to take time out to recharge. Go off gthe rid for a week. Play with your children. Walk on the beach with your spouse. Down time will shed light on why you are doing what you are doing in your "up time," and will keep you motivated over peaks and across valleys.

Are you excited to get started? Do you wake up ready to sprint to your business? Then you are in the right place, doing the right thing. Search your heart and soul, understand your vision and purpose, set your goals, maintain your work/life balance, and go for it. If you aren't ready to sprint, you are not doing what you love. If you aren't doing what you love, or if you race out the door without a roadmap, you will end up running in circles. Do what you love, do it for the right reasons, do it with a plan, and everyone around you will benefit.

I have written this book to spare readers some of the agony I went through in my earliest years of entrepreneurship. Over time, I have discovered what works and what doesn't. In closing, I invite all readers to visit my website EricCasaburi.com and download their very own GPS—that is, I extend to you the exact same Goals/Purpose/Success template I use on a daily basis.

Print out your GPS today; prioritize it; use it daily. Now that you have come to the end of this book, fill your next few steps with a sense of urgency. It is time to take action. Make a specific statement or promise or goal, and put it down on paper. Make one list of personal goals and one list of professional goals. Remember to ask yourself, "*Why* is this goal meaningful to me?"

And then get to it, because I'm here to tell you: Once you write your dreams and goals down, they become real. Organize your work and life goals together, so that they complement each other and fit like a puzzle. Do not let your personal goals run parallel to your professional goals; they must intersect, or you are doomed.

You can have both personal and professional success if you take to heart what I have laid out in these chapters. Use the

GPS I have created—write something on it tonight. I know thousands of people just like me who are winning in business and in life, and who are excited to get out of bed every morning. Tap into the spirit of entrepreneurship and live the life of your dreams.

NOTES _____

_____

_____

_____

_____

_____

_____

_____

_____

_____

_____

_____

_____

_____

_____

_____

_____

_____

_____

NOTES _____

NOTES _____

CPSIA information can be obtained at www.ICGtesting.com
Printed in the USA
BVOW04*1804040515

398884BV00004B/9/P